SPIES of MISSISSIPPI

SPIES of MISSISSIPPI

THE TRUE STORY OF THE SPY NETWORK THAT TRIED TO DESTROY THE CIVIL RIGHTS MOVEMENT

BY RICK BOWERS

NATIONAL GEOGRAPHIC

WASHINGTON, D.C.

The National Geographic Society is one of the world's largest nonprofit scientific and educational organizations. Founded in 1888 to "increase and diffuse geographic knowledge," the Society works to inspire people to care about the planet. It reaches more than 325 million people worldwide each month through its official journal, *National Geographic,* and other magazines; National Geographic Channel; television documentaries; music; radio; films; books; DVDs; maps; exhibitions; school publishing programs; interactive media; and merchandise. National Geographic has funded more than 9,000 scientific research, conservation and exploration projects and supports an education program combating geographic illiteracy. For more information, visit nationalgeographic.com.

For more information, please call 1-800-NGS LINE (647-5463)
or write to the following address:
National Geographic Society
1145 17th Street N.W.
Washington, D.C. 20036-4688 U.S.A.

Visit us online at www.nationalgeographic.com/books
For librarians and teachers: www.ngchildrensbooks.org
More for kids from National Geographic: kids.nationalgeographic.com

For information about special discounts for bulk purchases, please contact National Geographic Books Special Sales: ngspecsales@ngs.org

For rights or permissions inquiries, please contact National Geographic Books Subsidiary Rights: ngbookrights@ngs.org

Text design by Eva Absher

Library of Congress Cataloging-in-Publication Data

Bowers, Rick, 1952-
  The spies of Mississippi : the true story of the spy network that tried to destroy the civil rights movement / by Rick Bowers. – 1st ed.
     p. cm.
  Includes bibliographical references and index.
  ISBN 978-1-4263-0595-5 (hardcover : alk. paper) – ISBN 978-1-4263-0596-2 (library binding : alk. paper)
  1. Mississippi State Sovereignty Commission–History. 2. African Americans–Civil rights–Mississippi–History–20th century. 3. African Americans–Segregation–Mississippi–History–20th century. 4. States' rights (American politics)–History–20th century. 5. Mississippi–Politics and government–1951- 6. Mississippi–Race relations. 7. Civil rights movements–Mississippi–History–20th century. I. Title.
  E185.93.M6B69 2010
  323.1196'0730762–dc22

                        2009018944

Printed in the United States of America

09/WOR/1

TABLE OF CONTENTS

With profound love and joy
to Wynn, Neva, and Helen

ACKNOWLEDGMENTS
I wish to thank my wife, Wynn, for her constant support and
dedication to this endeavor. The compelling images in this book
are due to her expert and relentless research. Special thanks to
National Geographic editor Nancy Feresten, who immediately
recognized the power of the concept and steadfastly guided the
progress of the work. A special appreciation to the staff at the
Mississippi Department of Archives and History, who were always there to aid in the search for information and to open new
pathways to insight and understanding. In fact, throughout
the state, archivists, librarians, and historians openly shared
important pieces of the civil rights story under their purview.
Special thanks to friends who listened to the stories, provided
encouragement, and even helped with early ideas and edits.
Naturally, I offer a heartfelt thanks to the civil rights pioneers
who shared their memories with me. It was a profound honor
to hear their recollections of the past and to witness their continuing quest for justice.

FOREWORD

You are about to encounter the spies and counterspies, agents and double agents, informants and infiltrators of the Mississippi State Sovereignty Commission— the secret, state-funded spy program formed to stop the march toward equality and justice in the 1950s and 1960s. You will also encounter dedicated civil rights workers and fearless student activists, truth-telling journalists and justice-seeking lawyers who dared to challenge the status quo imposed by the seemingly all-powerful state. The United States was founded on the ideals of equal opportunity for all—white and black, Hispanic and Asian, gay and straight, old and young. Achieving these ideals demands constant vigilance to protect our civil liberties against unwarranted government intrusion in our private lives. Standing on the shoulders of those who came before, we are called upon to defend—and to extend—those essential civil and human rights.

Wade Henderson
President and CEO,
Leadership Conference on Civil Rights

PROLOGUE

Twelve of the most powerful men in the state controlled a secretive network of spies and informants.
A cadre of covert operatives used code names like Agent X, Agent Y, and Agent Zero. Neighbors spied on neighbors. Teachers spied on students. Ministers spied on churchgoers. Spies spied on spies. This is not the description of a Cold War–era secret police force or a futuristic sci-fi dictatorship. This government-run spy network infiltrated the lives of private citizens right here in the United States and not too long ago—in the state of Mississippi during the height of the civil rights movement of the 1950s and 1960s.

The Mississippi State Sovereignty Commission operated as a clandestine investigative arm of the state government for more than a decade. It compiled secret files on more than 87,000 private citizens and organizations. Staffed by a team of professional agents and funded by taxpayers, the commission had a fundamental mission: to save segregation at all costs. In the process, its agents carried out the most extensive state spying program in U.S. history.

How do we know all this is true? The Commission itself

tells us. The 134,000 pages and 87,000 names in its once-secret investigative file tell the story of its clandestine programs, its network of neighborhood informants, its brutal behind-the-scenes maneuvering, and its intervention in many of the most significant events of the civil rights era. In their own words, the agents reveal their tactics for infiltrating civil rights groups, forcing liberal college professors out of their jobs, collaborating with white racist organizations, and rewarding black leaders for supporting segregation.

The extensive investigative file does not tell the whole story, however. For this book, I've filled out the story with oral histories, personal memoirs, historical studies, academic dissertations, government documents, and newspaper and magazine articles from the era. In addition, I've traveled Mississippi—from the cotton fields in the Mississippi River Delta to the beach towns on the Gulf Coast to the capital of Jackson—interviewing people connected to the story. I've also uncovered surveillance documents and photographs, including a hand-drawn map showing the burial site of three murdered civil rights workers and photos of student protesters with red numbers scrawled next to their faces. Those numbers targeted the "subversives" for further investigation.

Despite the tracks left behind by the anti–civil rights spies and the excellent research and writing on the subject in Mississippi, the story remains largely unknown to the general public. It is usually relegated to a footnote in the history of the civil rights movement.

No longer.

This is how it happened.

1

THE GENESIS

At noon sharp on a bright, 43-degree day in January 1956, J. P. Coleman placed his right hand on his mother's Bible and took the oath to become the 51st governor of Mississippi. The 6-foot, 2-inch gentleman farmer, lawyer, and Civil War historian cast an impressive figure as he stood at the podium preparing to deliver his inaugural address. Coleman looked out over the 3,000 people gathered in the public square in the state capital of Jackson. Virtually all the faces looking back at him were white.

A segregationist and skilled public speaker, Coleman launched into his inaugural address, vowing to "maintain the continued separation of the white and Negro races." But aware that tensions between whites and blacks were threatening to flare into violence in a number of cities and towns across the state, Coleman also warned his audience—including both chambers of the state legislature and the state supreme court—that preserving segregation was "no task for the amateur or the hothead." When it came to the tense relationship between whites and blacks in Mississippi, Coleman wanted "peace and quiet." In Mississippi in 1956, that made him a moderate.

Once settled in to the governor's mansion, Coleman waded through a stream of bills coming to his desk from the state legislature, which was fixated on shoring up the walls of segregation. House Bill 880 caught his eye. It called for the creation of the Mississippi State Sovereignty Commission, a special agency that would preserve the state's "sovereignty"—that is, its right to govern itself without undue interference from the federal government or private pressure groups. The lawmakers behind the bill had made it clear that sovereignty was really just a high-minded code word for segregation—the official state policy of keeping the races separate and keeping whites in a position of power over blacks. The Commission would be granted extraordinary powers, including the power to investigate private citizens and organizations, to maintain secret files, to force witnesses to testify, and even to make arrests.

From a legal standpoint, Coleman worried that such a potent and secretive investigative agency could trample on the rights of private citizens. From a political standpoint, he knew that those powerful lawmakers would not back down until the bill was signed into law. And from a practical standpoint, he had to admit that having his own operatives to keep an eye on civil rights "agitators" could help to maintain his coveted racial peace and quiet. As the new governor signed the bill, he vowed to contain the agency's power by surrounding it with moderates like himself, instead of the outspoken, racist politicians and civic leaders he called "fire-eaters."

With the stroke of his pen, the Commission was born. Governor Coleman, despite his reluctance, became the overseer of the state's new segregation watchdogs.

CHAPTER 2

GROWING OUTRAGE, GROWING BACKLASH

The segregation watchdogs would have plenty to keep an eye on. From Gulfport to Greenville, civil rights activists had stepped up their boycotts, marches, prayer vigils, and demonstrations against segregation and discrimination, inequality and injustice. The catalyst had been the 1954 U.S. Supreme Court ruling in *Brown v. Board of Education*, which barred segregation in public schools and required states to integrate schools "with all deliberate speed." The ruling prompted more and more opponents of segregation to join the National Association for the Advancement of Colored People (NAACP), an interracial organization formed in 1909 to advocate for equal rights for African Americans. Now the NAACP was setting up local chapters in cities and towns throughout Mississippi—and the rest of the country—to push for integration.

The growing outrage of blacks was greeted with a growing backlash from many whites. The more extreme opponents of integration called for a campaign of "massive resistance" by white community leaders and ordinary citizens. City leaders barred demonstrations;

county sheriffs began jailing activists on trumped-up charges; the Ku Klux Klan awoke from a long slumber with cross burnings, beatings, and even murder.

Thousands of people were joining the newly formed White Citizens' Council, a self-described civic organization with a stated mission of defending segregation by legal means—and without violence. The movement was inspired by Mississippi Circuit Court Judge Thomas Pickens Brady, who published a handbook entitled *Black Monday*, which denounced the 1954 Supreme Court ruling, introduced a racist philosophy, and compared black people to cockroaches and chimpanzees. Brady called for the disbandment of the NAACP and proposed radical alternatives to integrated schools, including the abolition of all public schools and even the creation of a separate state for Negroes.

By the time Governor Coleman took office, the state was studded with White Citizens' Council chapters. Their leaders saturated their community newspapers with pro-segregation messages, advocated for tougher segregation ordinances, supported segregationist political candidates, and fiercely denounced the NAACP by calling it the National Association for the Agitation of Colored People. The Council's most effective weapon was the economic advantage that middle- and upper-class whites held over the majority of blacks. Council leaders got suspected civil rights sympathizers fired from their jobs, turned down for credit, forced out of business, or evicted from their homes. Behind the scenes, more than a few Council leaders resorted to threats, intimidation, and violence, as they worked hand in hand with the Klan.

Critics of the White Citizens' Council—noting that most of its leaders were respected white businessmen dressed in suits and ties rather than hoods and robes—dubbed the organization the "Country Club Klan." Liberal journalist Hodding Carter, editor of the crusading *Delta Democrat Times,* warned that the most extreme white racists would take control of the council. "When the pot boils," Carter said, "the scum rises to the top."

Most black Mississippians were not buying segregation, even if they had to keep their views to low whispers to avoid persecution. Many others were voting with their feet by moving north in search of better jobs and more tolerance. Still others, convinced that the entrenched white political class would never give up power, chose to make the best of it in a black-and-white world. Those few subservient blacks who played up to white authority figures in exchange for preferential treatment were branded Uncle Toms, a term drawn from a fictional character in Harriet Beecher Stowe's novel *Uncle Tom's Cabin*. The term, a badge of shame in the black community, suggested that the person was selling out his or her own people.

The Mississippi State Sovereignty Commission was counting on it.

CHAPTER 3

THE "BIBLE"

As the tension between the races simmered, Governor Coleman assumed the chairmanship of the board that would oversee the Sovereignty Commission. The 12 board members—including the powerful president of the Mississippi Senate, the speaker of the Mississippi House, and the state attorney general—would provide political cover for the agency's hidden operations. Once the board was in place, Coleman set up a propaganda unit to wage a war of words against the NAACP. The unit would produce and distribute pro-segregation messages, ultimately compiling a package of press releases, films, speeches, and testimonials that would become known as the "Bible."

Coleman appointed his former campaign publicity chief Hal DeCell to head up the unit. DeCell, editor of the weekly Deer Creek *Pilot* in the tiny delta town of Rolling Fork, had lobbied for a big public relations job with the state. He promised to repute the "vicious falsehoods" and "slanderous misrepresentation" coming from "antagonistic pressure groups," the federal government, and the "poisoned pens" of the elite Yankee press. As public relations chief, DeCell began crafting the story line that segregation was good for both whites and blacks, and that most "Negroes" in the Magnolia State actually preferred it. He started sending pro-segregation editorials to newspapers across the country, developing a pro-segregation film, and distributing pamphlets that painted a glowing portrait of race relations in the state. DeCell escorted northern newspaper editors on tours of the Mississippi River and excursions to the tourist towns on the Gulf Coast in an effort to show that whites and blacks lived and worked in carefully controlled harmony in segregated Mississippi.

As would be expected, DeCell's public relations package did not mention the state's long history of maintaining white dominance over blacks, which dated to the earliest days of slavery. At that time the state established rigid "slave codes" that defined African Americans as property, dictated the conditions of their captivity, and prescribed brutal punishments for the slightest infractions. Even after the Civil War and the abolition of slavery, the ruling class in Mississippi—and throughout the South—retained power by establishing new laws, customs, and punishments that bore a striking resemblance to the old slave codes.

The new "black codes" restricted freedoms of speech, travel, voting, owning land, and choosing an occupation. White supremacy—the concept that white people are naturally superior to blacks—was written into law, taught in schools, praised in churches, and reinforced in the media. The laws and customs that propped up white power were commonly referred to as Jim Crow, after an old, crippled black character portrayed by white minstrel show performers. With their faces blackened by charcoal or burned cork, the minstrel showmen danced a ridiculous jig and sang a mocking song titled "Jump Jim Crow," inadvertently putting a name to the degrading conditions that dominated the lives of African Americans.

The Mississippi State Sovereignty Commission had a plan to preserve Jim Crow. Its agents were going undercover.

CHAPTER 4

THE PIPELINE

As the Commission's propaganda machine ground out its self-serving distortions, Coleman decided to add to its arsenal. He began setting up a secret investigative unit that would be patterned after the FBI and U.S. military intelligence agencies during wartime, "seeking out intelligence information about the enemy and what the enemy proposed to do." Specifically, Coleman wanted a small team of investigators to infiltrate the NAACP and to keep him apprised of its plans to form new chapters, to organize protest demonstrations, to boycott businesses, and to file lawsuits.

The governor began hiring investigators and assigned them to develop a network of paid and unpaid informants to serve as the Commission's "eyes and ears" in communities statewide. The agents found willing collaborators in white civic leaders, businessmen, sheriffs, deputies, judges, and ministers. Determined to stop integration, the informants began calling the Commission's office in the New State Capitol Building in Jackson. They reported conversations overheard between "Negro agitators," rumors of upcoming protest actions, and the names and descriptions of suspected NAACP leaders in their midst. The Commission agents dubbed this network of neighborhood spies the "pipeline."

Building the white information pipeline was easy compared to the task of recruiting blacks to inform on other blacks. But as one Commission report would conclude, "This problem will never be solved without the help of the Negroes in the state of Mississippi." Seeking "a large number of fine, level-headed Negro citizens actively opposed to the NAACP," the agents began quietly soliciting conservative black community leaders to serve as confidential informants. They offered payments of $10 to $500 per assignment to keep tabs on suspicious neighbors or to join the NAACP and send its meeting notes, plans, and member lists to handlers at the Commission.

At first, most black informants were small-time operators, but in spring 1957, agents began cozying up to Percy Greene, editor and publisher of the *Jackson Advocate*, the black newspaper with the largest circulation in the state. The word was that the outspoken, cigar-chomping newspaperman was uneasy with the NAACP's demands for immediate school integration and felt out of step with its younger, more opinionated leaders. In addition, Greene needed cash to shore up his financially strapped weekly newspaper and wasn't choosy about his sources of income. The big-talking editor liked to brag that he'd take money from the devil if it meant selling more papers.

After a series of meetings with publicity chief DeCell,

Greene made good on his boast and formed a devil's bargain with the Commission. He would publish its propaganda in his newspaper and keep tabs on the NAACP. The Commission would cover his travel expenses to out-of-state meetings and funnel money to him under the guise of subscriptions, advertising, and printing jobs.

Greene hammered the NAACP in his columns and editorials, condemning its "vindictive speeches" against "responsible white people" and began funneling information to the Commission. And he made a handsome side income. In 1958 alone, Greene received $3,200 from the Commission—more than $31,000 in today's money.

Shortly after wooing and winning Greene, the spies scored an even bigger prize. Reverend Henry Harrison Humes—one of the most influential African-American ministers in the state—agreed to serve as a confidential informant. Rev. H. H. Humes was the longtime pastor of New Hope Baptist Church in Greenville, editor of the weekly *Delta Leader*, and president of the 387,000-member Baptist State Convention, the largest black Baptist organization in Mississippi. Now he was riding a circuit of black churches across the Mississippi River Delta and building a loyal following through his powerful oratory and moral decrees. Humes had significant influence over ordinary churchgoers, a powerful voice in church affairs, and plenty of contacts within the NAACP.

A conservative black preacher supporting segregation was rare but not completely unheard of in Mississippi at that time. White community leaders often bestowed special status on "Negro preachers" for keeping politics out of the pulpit and keeping their flocks focused on the rewards of the afterlife rather than the shortcomings of the here and now. Black ministers who toed the line received contributions to their church funds, special relationships with white community leaders, and even a voice in state affairs. Humes was cut from that cloth.

As an informant, Humes proved himself by providing intelligence on NAACP recruitment in his hometown of Greenville. His first check was for a modest $29.76 for "investigations." A February 11, 1957, memo recommended paying him $150 to spy on other black preachers at an upcoming regional ministerial meeting in Atlanta, because his report "could alert us to local situations." Now the preacher was in a position to ingratiate himself with the state, to undercut his rivals within the NAACP, and to make serious money.

Humes followed up the initial assignments with such detailed information and enticing leads that his handlers steadily upped his pay. Before long, the minister was receiving a $150 monthly salary and additional payments for special assignments. The 55-year-old preacher became the primary source of anti–civil rights intelligence in the Delta. He provided advance word on NAACP meetings, warnings of visits from out-of-state leaders, whispers of future actions, and the names and addresses of new members and aspiring leaders. Humes was so thorough that he even hired a stenographer to record

NAACP meetings word for word. He mailed meticulous reports to the Commission office and frequently drove to Jackson to brief his handlers in person.

Then, in July 1957, everything changed. Greene and Humes were exposed. The Associated Press broke a story stating that two black leaders were pocketing under-the-table payments from a public agency dedicated to preserving segregation. The proof: state-issued checks made out to Greene and Humes from the Sovereignty Commission.

The civil rights community was outraged by the betrayal. NAACP leaders complained that their work to secure equal rights for ordinary people had been jeopardized by a couple of well-heeled Uncle Toms. Grassroots activists grumbled that they were going to jail for the cause while well-to-do community members were on the payroll of the jailers. The leadership of the NAACP fired back at the informants. NAACP executive director Roy Wilkins told a packed crowd of 600 people at the Mount Bethel Baptist Church in Gulfport that Greene and Humes were "quick to get their hands in the till."

Speaking from the pulpit of the same church in Gulfport, Humes denied the allegations. Addressing hundreds of people packed into the pews, he charged that the NAACP had "fallen into bad hands." But Humes's supporters were slow to rally to his defense, and his enemies were quick on the attack. NAACP members circulated a petition calling for his removal as president of the Baptist Convention. A coalition of black preachers issued a statement calling him "unworthy of the fellowship of the ministers of the Protestant denominations in Mississippi."

Deflated by the attacks and fearful of being exposed again by reporters, Humes cut back on his spying and stopped traveling to Jackson to file reports. Instead he met his handlers at secret locations to plead for their support in clearing his name. He became consumed by the vendetta against him and depressed about his fall from grace.

Then, one night while driving home from a friend's house, Humes started to feel sick. Concerned that his condition was worsening, he made his way to a segregated medical clinic to be examined. While waiting to be tended to, the minister went into a seizure, suffered a heart attack, and died. The next day Humes's Commission contact sent a memo to Governor Coleman. It read, "The death of Rev. Humes has cost us one of the most influential Negroes we have had working on our behalf." Later, the agent drove to the minister's house in Greenville and, unbeknownst to the grieving family, slipped into Humes's office "to remove all files dealing with the Sovereignty Commission."

The exposure of the black informants lifted a curtain on the state's secret spy network. Now, NAACP leaders were keenly aware of the dangers posed by those curious men in suits who had been jotting down the tag numbers of

cars parked outside their meeting places. Civil rights
activists began taking steps to protect their confidential
documents and calling out suspected snitches in their
meetings. For its part, the Commission quickly replaced
Humes with one of his followers and added more informants—white and black—to its intelligence pipelines.
As for Greene, he weathered the storm and continued
informing and publishing propaganda. The two sides
were poised for conflict, and there was more controversy
bubbling up from the rich, black Mississippi River Delta.

CHAPTER 5

THE DELTA BLUES

The Mississippi River Delta is a study in contrast.
The vast stretches of green and white cotton fields are
interspersed with eerie, moss-draped cypress swamps.
The white-pillared mansions of the plantation elite stand
near the huts of the poor dirt farmer. The Delta is home
to debutante balls and backroom gambling dens, ram-
shackle houseboats and majestic paddle wheelers. This
sweltering, insect-ridden, and amazingly fertile stretch
of bottomland forms, in the words of author James C.
Cobb, "the most Southern place on earth."

Back in the 1860s, hundreds of thousands of slaves
worked the vast cotton fields. They were afraid to resist
or to run for fear of being whipped, beaten, or sold away
from their families. Each day, more black men, women,
and children were delivered to the plantations by slave
brokers, who purchased their human cargo in the bustling markets of New Orleans and Natchez and marched
them in groups of about 30 for hundreds of miles to their
oppressive new homes. The seemingly endless supply
of slave labor and a ravenous demand for cotton fueled a
robust economy dominated by wealthy planters, powerful politicians, and influential businessmen.

The legacy of slavery, the grip of poverty, and widespread illiteracy made it virtually impossible for civil rights workers to organize effectively in the Delta prior to the 1950s. The small cotton-processing towns and thinly populated enclaves seemed destined to be racially segregated and brutally oppressive for African Americans for generations to come. But by the late 1950s, in the hardscrabble river town of Clarksdale, change was in the air. Aaron Henry, president of the Coahoma County Chapter of the NAACP and executive secretary of the Regional Council of Negro Leadership, was organizing the black community. The mild-mannered activist was petitioning the local school board to integrate schools, urging the sheriff to crack down on the harassment of black voters, and demanding that newspaper editors refer to black people in their columns with the courtesy titles of Mr., Mrs., and Miss.

Henry, a registered pharmacist and owner of the Fourth Street Drug Store, had turned his pharmacy into a makeshift community center and citizenship school, where he prepared poor sharecroppers, shopkeepers, and household servants to vote for the first time. Affectionately known in the community as Doc, Henry had a unique ability to work across the racial divide and a talent for forming unlikely alliances.

Henry had grown up in a sharecropping family on the Flowers Brothers Plantation outside Clarksdale. He escaped poverty by joining the army and learned his pharmacy craft at Xavier College in New Orleans. After college, drawn by the lure of the land and a determination to end racial prejudice, he returned home to the

Delta. "You know that old Mississippi River has never had an ounce of racial prejudice," he liked to say. "When it comes to bursting over those levees, it doesn't stop to ask where the colored section is. It just takes all."

The Commission spies initially underestimated Henry's effectiveness. They bragged of duping him into divulging valuable information without even knowing it. But over time, Henry's relentless organizing and alliance building forced the spies to enhance their surveillance. In early 1958, Commission agent Zach Van Landingham traveled to Clarksdale to meet three men—a judge, a candidate for sheriff, and a leader of the Clarksdale chapter of the White Citizens' Council. The prominent local leaders told the agent that the pharmacist-turned-organizer was stirring up needless trouble in the black community and laid out a plan to rid themselves of the agitator.

The Council would pressure wholesalers to stop selling supplies to Henry's drugstore and would press doctors to refuse to write prescriptions for patients who shopped there. The economic squeeze would bankrupt Henry and force him to leave town in search of work. The Council also planned to persuade the superintendent of the Coahoma Country Negro School District to fire Henry's wife, Nicole, from her teaching job just to make sure the couple had no reason to stay in town. "It is believed that if Henry leaves the area," Van Landingham reported to his superiors at the Commission, "the NAACP will die."

The Commission surrounded Henry with black informants, who infiltrated his meetings and intercepted his documents. One report noted that an informant code-named J1 "advised that he had been listening very closely in his church," and it appeared that NAACP meetings were "not well attended" and that Henry was not "doing very well with his drugstore." But Henry kept holding meetings, signing up members, registering voters, and speaking out in the press. NAACP membership and black voter registration in the region crept upward.

Then, late in 1958, Henry was elected president of the Mississippi branch of the NAACP, thus becoming one of the most important civil rights leaders in the state. He forged alliances with multiple civil rights organizations, developed relationships with federal authorities, and made friends with sympathetic journalists.

Despite the recognition and the stature, his struggle was really just beginning. After the mayor and Chamber of Commerce of Clarksdale moved to ban blacks from participating in the 1961 Christmas parade, Henry launched a boycott of white-owned businesses, with the slogan, "If we can't parade downtown, we won't trade downtown." The boycott triggered an unprecedented three-year reign of terror against the black community. During that time, Henry's wife was fired from her teaching job, his drugstore was firebombed, his house was torched, and he was arrested and jailed on false charges. As punishment, he was tied to the back of a garbage truck and forced to load trash in full view of his neighbors. But the attempt to humiliate him backfired on his tormentors. The sight of an unrelenting freedom worker tethered to a trash truck only enhanced his stature in the black community.

6

DEATH OF A DREAM

Clyde Kennard climbed into his 1958 Mercury station wagon and drove from the black farming hamlet of Eatonville to the stately, all-white campus of Mississippi Southern College. The pristine campus, with its redbrick walkways, white-columned buildings, and shimmering lily ponds, seemed a world away from the family poultry farm that he was running for his ailing mother.

The former U.S. Army paratrooper and University of Chicago political science major was headed to the office of Mississippi Southern president W. D. McCain to get word on his application to enroll at the college. The 30-year-old Kennard was all too aware that he had stirred up a hornet's nest by applying to an all-white public college, but he had no idea that he was walking into a setup of epic proportions. Commission investigator Zach Van Landingham was waiting for Kennard in President McCain's office—as was a formal letter of rejection. The police were also watching and waiting with dangerous intentions in mind. The Commission's role in his undoing would prove that its extraordinary powers were far beyond the point of being contained.

SPIES of MISSISSIPPI

Clyde Kennard was born on June 12, 1927, and raised among the cotton and corn fields of rural Forrest County, Mississippi. At age 12, his family sent him to live with his sister in Chicago so he would have a chance to attend decent schools. In 1945 Kennard enlisted in the army. He graduated from paratrooper school, served as a paratrooper in Korea and Germany, and rose to the rank of sergeant. In 1952, he received an honorable discharge, with the Bronze Star, Korean Service Medal, United Nations Service Medal, and Good Conduct Medal to his credit.

After his discharge, Kennard earned a high school diploma, began taking college courses, and enrolled full-time at the University of Chicago. He completed two years toward a political science degree. Then he got bad news: His stepfather was dying, and his mother couldn't keep up the farm. In spring 1954, at age 28, Kennard left the University of Chicago for the family chicken farm in Mississippi.

Kennard applied for admission to Mississippi Southern in 1956. His application was denied as incomplete. He reapplied in 1958. It was denied again for alleged ir-regularities. Then, late in 1959, Kennard applied again. This time he explained his decision—and openly mocked the concept of a segregated society—in an editorial in the *Hattiesburg American:* "Are we to assume that two sets of hospitals are to be built for two groups of doctors? Are we to build two bridges across the same stream to give equal opportunity to two groups of engineers? Are we to have two courts of law so as to give both groups of lawyers the same chance to demonstrate their skills; two legislatures for our politically inclined; and of course two governors?" Regarding integration and racial cooperation, Kennard concluded, "I would rather meet my God with this creed than with any other yet devised by human society."

Suddenly, the army veteran, college student, and poultry farmer had captured public attention. The national press jumped on the story of a black military veteran seeking to break the color barrier in higher education in Mississippi. The NAACP offered legal assistance in case Kennard decided to sue the college to gain admission. And the next entry in the Commission's secret file read in understated fashion, "The Clyde Kennard problem is no longer simply a local concern."

Agent Van Landingham began working up an investigation, relying on the initial groundwork provided by a confidential investigator code-named T1. The exhaustive probe examined Kennard's childhood in Hattiesburg, his upbringing in Chicago, his years in the military, in college, and on the farm. The agents interviewed his friends, teachers, ministers, and business associates and sent a bank examiner to the Citizens' Bank of Hattiesburg to inspect his accounts. The search turned up nothing that undercut his application. "Persons who know Kennard describe him as intelligent, well educated, quiet spoken, courteous with a desire to better the Negro race," Van Landingham reported.

The investigators were so intent on finding damn-
ing information that their reports presented the most
mundane facts with sinister implication. The agents
noted that as a student Kennard joined the Progressive
Citizens' Club and the German Club. Furthermore, "the
files of confidential agent T1 reflect that Clyde Kennard
has no middle name."

With little to go on, Van Landingham paid a visit to
Dudley W. Conner, head of the White Citizens' Council
of Hattiesburg. Without prodding, Conner offered to
have his Council henchmen "take care of [Kennard]."
When pressed by the investigator on the meaning
behind that menacing statement, Conner explained,
"Kennard's car could be hit by a train or he could have
some accident on the highway and no one would ever
know the difference."

As an alternative to the Council's extreme approach,
Van Landingham devised a more moderate plan to
pressure Kennard to drop his application. As part of that
plan, Governor Coleman invited Kennard to a meeting in
Jackson and offered to get him into a segregated Negro
college or even an integrated university in the North.
Short of that, the governor appealed to Kennard to
hold off on his application until the controversy over it
"cooled down," maybe after the next election.

Van Landingham also organized a committee of
influential black educators to lobby Kennard to drop his
application. The educators agreed to make the case in
exchange for the governor's support for a state-funded
Negro junior college in Hattiesburg. Pleading with
Kennard to take back the application, they warned that

his attempt to become the first black admitted to an all-white college could undercut black schools and lead to trouble, even bloodshed.

Kennard refused to back down. Now, for him, it was a matter of principle. He even questioned the role of the investigators on his trail. "Is it the integrationists or segregationists who are employing secret investigators to search records?" he asked.

The fateful meeting between Kennard and Mississippi Southern president McCain was set for Tuesday, September 14, 1959, at 9:30 a.m. The entire meeting lasted just 20 minutes. McCain and Van Landingham implored Kennard to give up, but he politely held his ground. Then Mississippi Southern admissions director Aubrey Lucas was called into the office to hand Kennard the official letter of rejection, which claimed that his University of Chicago transcripts were incomplete and that his physical examination records had been altered, proving that he lacked the moral character to attend the prestigious college.

Kennard was escorted out of the office and back toward his car. In the distance he saw two campus police officers standing next to his vehicle. Constables Charlie Ward and Lee Daniels confronted him, accused him of speeding through the campus, and placed him under arrest for reckless driving. As one of the constables took Kennard into custody, the other apparently opened the station wagon and planted five half-pints of liquor under the front seat. Later that day, Kennard was charged with reckless driving and possession of liquor. At that time Mississippi was a dry state, and possessing liquor was technically illegal even though it was sold openly and was widely available.

After learning of the arrest, Van Landingham called the governor's office with the news. He told Coleman's administrative assistant, "It appeared to be a frame up with the planting of evidence in his car."

THE SAVIOR OF SEGREGATION

Throughout his campaign for governor, Ross Barnett traveled the state stoking the fears of small-town white voters with racially charged stump speeches. His voice moved from soft cadence to rolling thunder as he warned that their "cherished way of life" was being threatened by the "integrationists, agitators, subversives, and race mixers." "I am a Mississippi segregationist and proud of it," Barnett said to wild cheers. The crowds whooped, stomped their feet, and shouted back, "You tell 'em, Ross."

Barnett had lost two previous campaigns for governor, but this time he had an added advantage. The successful private attorney and former Klansman had been handpicked and endorsed by the White Citizens' Council, which had become a powerful political force in the state in a few short years. In fact, as Barnett picked up the pace of his campaign in 1959, the Council had more than 200 chapters with more than 80,000 members in Mississippi.

On the campaign trail, Barnett zeroed in on the federal government. The 1954 Supreme Court school desegregation ruling had been just the beginning of a

steady federal assault on segregation. The U.S. Justice
Department had formed a special division to make sure
the states enforced a growing body of civil rights laws.
Congress was considering sweeping new legislation
to mandate integration in public buildings, parks, and
playgrounds and to ban racial discrimination in the
workplace. Furthermore, a young, liberal Massachusetts
congressman named John F. Kennedy was running
for President. For the first time, a viable candidate for
the nation's highest office was courting the black vote.
Barnett knew change was coming. He also knew that
fear of that change was his ticket to power.

Barnett told voters that the national politicians were
trampling on Mississippi's right to govern itself. His
campaign workers even nailed posters to telephone poles
in small towns warning that only he could stop "the
occupation forces from the N.A.A.C.P. and the specially
trained goon squads from the Justice Department."

With his arms waving and his voice trembling, he
pledged that no public school, park, swimming pool, or
restroom would be integrated on his watch. And in the
end, this fierce segregationist, with a flair for drama
that would become his hallmark, summed up his position on integration with one word: "Never!" Standing
on the campaign stage, he would proclaim segregation
forever, and his hillbilly band would break into song,
"He's for segregation one hundred percent / He's not a
moderate, like some other gent."

Barnett also criticized departing governor Coleman
for failing to use the Commission to neutralize the
enemy. The fact that Barnett had no knowledge of the

Commission's secret operations didn't stop him from charging the segregation watchdogs with sleeping on the job.

Since Governor Coleman was ineligible to run for a consecutive second term under state law, Lieutenant Governor J. Carroll Gartin opposed Barnett in the key Democratic primary. And since the Republican Party had no viable candidate to run in the general election, the winner of the Democratic primary was certain to become governor. Gartin, a moderate on race in the Coleman tradition, could not rile up as much segregationist fervor as his demagogic rival. By the time the primary was held in August 1959, Barnett was gaining momentum, and he ended up winning by a comfortable margin. Upon hearing the news of Barnett's victory, outgoing Governor Coleman said, "May the good Lord help us for the next four years." With that, Ross Barnett rode a wave of white fear into the governor's mansion.

CHAPTER 8

THE CLANDESTINE WAR

"At all costs." Ross Barnett used that phrase to describe the lengths to which he would go in his efforts to preserve segregation in his native state. Delivering his inaugural address on a cold, gray day in January 1960, the new governor struck a tone of determination and defiance.

"You know and I know," he reassured his fellow white citizens, "that we will maintain segregation in Mississippi at all costs." The small-town boy who dreamed of growing up to become an important man had realized his greatest ambition. Barnett would relish the architectural excesses of the governor's mansion (he would install gold-plated fixtures in the bathrooms). He would take pride in the State Capitol Building, with its 16 different kinds of marble and its bronze statue of former governor and U.S. senator Theodore Bilbo, an openly racist and corrupt powermonger who proudly referred to himself as the Man.

Now Ross Barnett was the new man—and his rise to power proved that classic race baiting could still win elections in the Magnolia State.

After settling in to his office, Barnett received regular status reports, investigative memos, and personal briefings on the Commission and attended regular meetings of its governing board. The new governor expected the spies to wage a real clandestine war against the civil rights movement. But how? He had no set of directions for building a secret police force and no owner's manual for running a covert spy network. He was just a hardworking and successful farmer-turned-lawyer from the farming hamlet of Standing Pine.

One of ten sons of a Confederate Civil War veteran, Barnett had grown up vying for attention and developed an obsessive dream of wearing fine suits, making important speeches, and being in the limelight. He had worked his way through law school, built a successful law practice, and become president of the Mississippi Bar Association. Finally he rose to power as a classic white supremacist who once proclaimed, "God is the ultimate segregationist. He made the white man white and the Negro black and never intended them to mix."

But behind his back, people did not always give Barnett the respect he longed for. He was often mocked as a chronic bumbler, and his actions frequently added to the snickers. Speaking at a breakfast meeting with Jewish community leaders at a local synagogue, he thanked the members of B'nai Brith for joining him in "fine Christian fellowship." He once injured himself on an airport tarmac by stepping into the whirling propeller blade of his own campaign airplane. He would become the only governor to name two Miss Americas honorary colonels in the Mississippi National

Guard. Barnett liked to say, "I love mockingbirds, Miss Americas, and Mississippi."

Barnett's antics hid his raw intelligence, ambition, and persistence in his quest for power. He knew how to charm his friends and disarm his enemies with his courtly demeanor, down-home storytelling, quick wit, and lowbrow humor. He also knew how power worked and applied that knowledge to transforming the Commission. With the support of the state legislature, he doubled the Commission's budget and increased its staff. He fired an investigator who had chafed at Barnett's campaign claim of the Commission's foot-dragging, which had sent a clear message that the "moderate" course of the Coleman years was over. Barnett also stacked the Commission board with political allies who shared his views on race. Through his first year in office, Barnett and his allies took several steps to transform the agency into a more effective weapon of information war.

Step I: Enlist Powerful Allies

In a controversial move, Barnett pressed state officials to allow the Commission to funnel taxpayer dollars directly into the coffers of the White Citizens' Council. The Commission funding would begin at $5,000 a month for a speakers' program and total more than $200,000 over a number of years—more than $1.8 million in today's currency. And with the added legitimacy of public funding, the Council would position itself as a quasi-official arm of state government as it pushed its way into other state agencies, acquired confidential government information, collaborated with law enforcement, and demanded more and more power.

Step 2: Know Your Enemies

The Commission added a new director of investigations and a number of new agents to its roster while increasing its use of private detective agencies and "special" freelance operatives. The typical investigator was a former FBI agent or state police investigator with surveillance experience and a commitment to segregation. Under Barnett, the agents' investigative tactics became more aggressive and their reports increasingly mean-spirited, reflecting their personal opposition to integration and their disdain for their adversaries.

Step 3: Dehumanize the Opposition

The revitalized team immediately launched an extensive "subversive hunt," investigating private citizens for criticizing state officials, belonging to liberal organizations, or supporting unpopular causes. A report issued in March 1961 noted that investigations were being launched against people who were merely speaking out, people whose "utterances or actions indicate they should be watched with suspicion of future racial attitudes."

The investigative files increasingly referred to the opposition as agitators, subversives, beatniks, do-gooders, and Communists. The communist tag was the

most potent weapon even though it had been several
years since the fall from grace of U.S. senator Joseph
McCarthy of Wisconsin, whose finger-pointing ruined
reputations, wrecked careers, and led to his expulsion
from the Senate. In Mississippi, a person accused of being a communist was prejudged a supporter of the Soviet
Union at a time when that totalitarian, nuclear-armed
nation was aligning its allies against the United States.

Step 4: Control the Media

Barnett named his former campaign publicist Erle
Johnston the Commission's public relations director.
The former newspaper reporter, editor, and publisher
had solid ties to journalists in the Mississippi press. He
also knew how the national media worked and had con-
nections at national news services in Washington, D.C.,
and TV networks in New York. Johnston was the perfect
choice to work both sides of the story. He would adeptly
paint the Commission as a benign public relations operation representing the positive side of race relations in
the state. Behind the scenes, he would fine-tune the propaganda bible, emphasizing the soft sell of segregation.
"This is a selling job and it cannot be done by waving
red flags or using emotional approaches," he advised.
"Facts, situations, and an appeal for understanding will
be more effective in gaining support for the South."

Johnston expanded the propaganda package to
include carefully crafted speeches, articles by black segregationists, and a 27-minute film entitled *The Message
of Mississippi,* which "showed in scenes and interviews

the racial harmony that exists among the vast majorities
of each race."

Step 5: Set Moral Standards

The revitalized team launched a campaign to remove
"subversive" books from the shelves of schools and
public libraries. The Commission's education and information unit listed books that contained sections on
desegregation or labor organizations as unacceptable
and suggested replacing them with books that advocated segregation and white supremacy. At dozens of
colleges and high schools, it presented programs detail-
ing the evils of communism and loaned books, films, and
speeches on racial separation and white supremacy to
young readers.

CHAPTER 9

NEVER, NEVER LAND

Federal judge John Minor Wisdom coined a phrase for the political climate in Mississippi. Wisdom said that segregationist policy was crafted and defended in the "eerie atmosphere of never never land." A swipe at the segregationist cries of "Never," the remark also referred to James M. Barrie's classic children's novel *Peter Pan*, where children are led into a bizarre fantasy world—an alternate reality. The comparison to Mississippi was apropos. The deep racial divide, widespread poverty, and isolation kept Mississippi in a sort of social time warp. Mississippi had no major cosmopolitan center like Atlanta, New Orleans, or Memphis, where large newspapers carried competing points of view and major universities debated new ideas. When commercial airliners circled to land at the Jackson airport, pilots playfully instructed passengers to fasten their seat belts and set their watches back 50 years.

The fundamentals of segregation only began to describe the complicated world that Mississippians—approximately 55 percent white and 45 percent black—had to navigate at the time. A black woman was allowed to shop in a white-owned department store but could not try on clothes because the dressing rooms were reserved for whites only. A black child could be admitted into a public hospital but could not play with white children in the waiting area of the pediatrics ward. Black men and women were expected to respect white people at all times but were not to be addressed as Mr., Mrs., or Miss by whites. Both whites and blacks loved to attend the big event of the year: the Mississippi State Fair. It lasted for two weeks each summer—one week for white patrons and one week for "colored" patrons. These complex lines had to be understood and adhered to or very carefully sidestepped.

As the civil rights crusaders pressed for change, the white power structure pulled back hard to maintain the lines of demarcation. And with Barnett in the governor's office, the state moved toward an even stronger form of white resistance, doling out punishment to anyone who was found to be crossing the color line.

The harsher tactics also played a role in the continuing saga of Clyde Kennard, the military veteran who had been denied admission to all-white Mississippi Southern College. Kennard, who had been framed by the police for possession of liquor, soon found himself in another run-in with the law. This chapter in the saga began when the Forrest County Cooperative warehouse was burglarized. The day before, 19-year-old Johnny Lee Roberts had been loading trucks and had purposely left a door to the warehouse unlocked. The next morning, Roberts reentered the building and stole five bags of chicken feed worth $25. In short order, police grilled and arrested Roberts. Under pressure to confess, Roberts claimed that his friend, Clyde Kennard, had put him up to it.

Police searched Kennard's farm and came back with a couple of empty feed bags. Kennard was charged as an accomplice to burglary—a felony. On the witness stand, Roberts gave a meandering, hard-to-follow account of the robbery that confused even the district attorney. Still, it took an all-white jury only ten minutes to hand down guilty verdicts. Roberts got a suspended sentence, and the co-op rehired him. Kennard, by contrast, was sentenced to the maximum penalty—seven years of hard labor at the notorious Mississippi State Penitentiary at Parchman.

How bad was Parchman? The prison farm, constructed after the Civil War as a direct response to the abolition of slavery, was originally designed to instill young, wayward black men with the discipline that the whips of slave owners could no longer administer.

At the maximum security penitentiary, Kennard worked from sunup to sundown on the prison cotton farm. He urged his mother not to visit—"just make believe I'm back in the army." He spent Sundays writing letters for illiterate prisoners.

The NAACP worked without success to overturn Kennard's conviction but did manage to publicize his plight. Then, after two years of hard time, Kennard doubled over with stomach pain. He was rushed to the hospital and diagnosed with intestinal cancer. Doctors operated immediately, but the cancer had spread too far. The doctors recommended that Kennard be released, given "the extremely poor prognosis in this rather young patient." But Governor Barnett, determined to send a message to any would-be integrationists, refused to grant clemency. Barnett ordered that the dying man be returned to prison, where he was sent back into the cotton fields.

With Kennard's condition worsening, an outcry built up in the northern black press. Black comedian Dick Gregory, who had gained celebrity status entertaining white and black nightclub audiences and appearing on national TV, charged that the military veteran, college student, and chicken farmer had been framed, railroaded into prison, abused, neglected, and left for dead.

OVERFLOWING THE JAILS

—May 24, 1961—

I'm taking a ride on the Greyhound bus line
I'm taking a ride to Jackson this time
Hallelujah I'm a traveling
Hallelujah, ain't it fine
Hallelujah I'm a traveling
Down freedom's main line

The jittery road warriors sat in the red, silver, and white double-decker bus racing down Highway 80 in Alabama en route to Jackson, Mississippi. The freedom riders had to accept the fact that attacks on the bus were possible, even likely, despite the extraordinary police and military protection deployed to prevent violence. As the bus raced past the Alabama country-side, eight National Guardsmen with grim faces and bayonet-tipped rifles stood sentinel over the passengers, including ten newsmen and more than a dozen freedom riders. Sixteen police cars formed an escort, helicopters hovered overhead, and an L19 reconnaissance aircraft kept watch from higher above. As the bus reached the borderline sign reading "Welcome to the Magnolia

State," one rider quipped, "I'm going out of America, into a foreign country." Freedom Ride coordinator Diane Nash had to take a deep breath. After all, she had resisted calls to abandon the ride to Jackson, insisting that the movement could not succeed if the mere threat of mob violence could stop nonviolent protest.

As the caravan raced forward, Mississippi National Guardsmen fanned out along a wooded stretch of the route. They had been alerted to a tip that Klansmen planned to dynamite the bus shortly after it crossed the state line. Driving through stop signs and traffic lights, the convoy finally reached the city limits of Jackson and rolled to its destination: the interstate bus terminal. The time had come for the long-awaited showdown between the young activists and the Jackson City Police.

The protesters bounded off the bus and walked quickly toward the terminal. The black riders headed to the "whites only" waiting room, and the two white riders headed to the room marked "Negroes only." Jackson police issued two warnings and began making arrests. The police ran the protesters through a gauntlet of officers to waiting paddy wagons and shuttled them off to the local lockup. The first Freedom Ride to Mississippi of summer 1961 had been carried out in perfect choreography. Federal officials, state officials, freedom riders, and police breathed a sigh of relief. Violence had been avoided. At that time, none of them knew that waves of additional buses with hundreds of new riders would soon be en route to Jackson to repeat the process again, and again, and again.

Three weeks earlier, freedom riders had boarded

buses in Washington, D.C., determined to expose segregated waiting rooms, restrooms, and water fountains
in bus and train stations. The U.S. Supreme Court had
barred segregation in interstate travel in 1960, but the
ruling was being ignored south of the Mason-Dixon
Line. As the freedom riders moved into the Deep South,
white mobs were waiting with insults, threats, bottles,
and rocks. Then, outside Anniston, Alabama, an angry
mob firebombed a bus and beat the fleeing riders with
chains and baseball bats. In Birmingham, a club-wield-
ing mob attacked a bus just two blocks from the police
station, with police nowhere in sight to keep the peace.

In light of the violence, protest organizers with the
Congress of Racial Equality (CORE) prepared to call
a halt to the rides. Then, U.S. attorney general Robert
Kennedy brokered a deal with officials in Alabama and
Mississippi. The state officials promised to provide protection for the riders if local police could arrest protesters for breach of peace. That's when a group of young
activists from the newly formed Student Nonviolent
Coordinating Committee (SNCC, pronounced "Snick")
volunteered to make the trip to Jackson. The daring mission was undertaken by a new style of activist personi-
fied by Diane Nash, who was younger, more insistent,
and seemingly fearless in the face of danger. Convinced
that postponing defeat meant empowering the opposition, the freedom riders set out down a dangerous road.
The eyes of the nation and the world—stunned by the
news accounts of the Alabama attacks and shocked that
young students would put their lives on the line—were
focused on the drama. All eyes were on Mississippi.

Governor Barnett, the Mississippi Highway
Patrol, the Jackson City Police, and the Sovereignty
Commission were waiting with a plan. From their point
of view, the best course was to avert violence—along with
the negative, worldwide press coverage it would spawn.
The police planned to break up white crowds before they
became mobs, to arrest protesters without brutality, and
to charge them with simple breach of peace instead of
violation of segregation laws. In all likelihood, the local
courts would issue suspended sentences and modest
fines, and the freed students would return home with
the northern reporters close behind.

Behind the scenes, the Commission agents would
create files on the freedom riders, including their names,
addresses, organizational ties, and mug shots. The
investigators would run background checks in the riders'
home states in search of information that could be used to
discredit the movement as "subversive and Communist."
The files would be shared with law enforcement agencies in other southern states and used to identify repeat
offenders. If all went according to plan, the Commission's
propaganda machine would churn out the story that
Mississippi whites had not resorted to violence and
Mississippi blacks had not joined the protests, thus proving that segregation was key to peaceful race relations.

Not surprisingly, all did not go according to their
plan. Two weeks into the saga, the first wave of riders
was taken to court for an arraignment hearing. Judge
James Spencer found the students guilty and issued
$200 fines and 60-day suspended sentences. At that
point, the young and idealistic riders rewrote the script.

Determined to keep the spotlight on segregation by "filling the jails to overflowing," the riders refused to admit their guilt or to pay their fines. The white riders were returned to the relatively modern Jackson City Jail, while black prisoners went to the grim Hinds County Jail. And with dozens of students boarding Jackson-bound buses and trains, the goal of filling the jails looked attainable.

A month into the stalemate, the state introduced its response to jail overcrowding. Groups of prisoners were herded from their cells and loaded on gray vans with metal seats and barred windows. The vans drove out of town and into the country. The landscape moved from green hills to vast, flat stretches of green and white cotton fields and creepy cypress swamps. Some 140 miles into the trip, the riders looked through the barred windows and glimpsed a frightening scene. Prison inmates in black-and-white-striped garb chopped cotton in the fields under the gaze of guards on horseback with rifles draped over their arms. In the distance stood the barbed-wire fences and looming guard towers of the maximum security penitentiary at Parchman. The van crawled through the gate and into the inner core of the prison, stopping at the maximum-security unit that housed death row inmates, solitary confinement cells, and the electric chair.

The students were marched down grim walkways to even darker cell blocks. The men were led to cells adjacent to other inmates; the women were taken to an isolated unit. All were issued prison clothes, a Bible, an aluminum cup, and a toothbrush. For the first two days, the inmates lived in fear of being beaten by the guards—or "screws"—until it became clear that their national media status was assuring them hands-off treatment.

Confined to the maximum-security unit with only their Bibles to read, the riders passed the time singing freedom songs. The warden and guards—concerned that the soulful melodies and defiant lyrics could inspire other inmates to join in—repeatedly ordered the singers to stop. When the singing continued, the guards began taking away items of clothing, toothbrushes, and mattresses.

CORE organizer James Farmer recalled one singer's response: "He said: 'Come take my mattress. I'll keep my soul.' And everybody started singing, 'Ain't gunna let no body turn me 'round, turn me 'round, turn me 'round.'"

One night the guards introduced a new tactic by removing screens from the cell-block windows. Swarms of mosquitoes flowed into the cells. And worse was on the way: "A guard came in and said, 'Look at all them bugs. We're gunna have to spray,'" recalled freedom rider David Frankhauser. "Shortly thereafter, we heard what sounded like a large diesel truck pull up outside the cell block. And what looked like a fire hose was passed in through one of the high windows. As the engine fired up outside, we were hit with a powerful spray of DDT. Being trapped in our cells, with no protection, our bodies, and every inch of the cells, were drenched with the eye-stinging, skin-burning insecticide."

Five weeks into the summer stalemate, more than 150 freedom riders had been arrested and convicted,

and waves of additional buses were en route to Jackson.
Northern newspaper accounts of alleged abuses at
Parchman prompted demands that independent delega-
tions be allowed to inspect conditions and interview the
prisoners. Mississippi officials needed a bold new story
to change the headlines.

Commission publicity director Erle Johnston had headed north in an effort to persuade skeptical audiences
that all was returning to normal in Jackson. In late
June, he told a gathering at the Rotary Club in Pocatello,
Idaho, that the "self-styled" freedom riders had "failed"
to reveal a dark side to southern segregation. To the
contrary, Johnston claimed, riders had "brought many
representatives of the news media into Mississippi who
were able to learn firsthand how the two races work and
live in harmony." Looking his audience in the eye, the
public relations man claimed that the riders had inadvertently "done the state a service."

At about that time, Commission investigator Andy
Hopkins began corresponding with R. J. Strickland,
chief investigator of the Florida Legislative Investigative
Committee. The two were members of a coalition of
southern law enforcement investigators who shared
information and tactics for fighting "subversion."
Strickland supplied Hopkins—a graduate of the FBI
training academy—with a four-page document entitled
"Fair Play for Cuba." It contained the names of 202
people who had allegedly flown to Havana, Cuba, four
months earlier. Two names on the list—compiled from

flight manifests at Miami International Airport—were those of freedom riders arrested in Jackson. Was their visit to Cuba—an island nation off the coast of Florida and a communist ally of the Soviet Union—proof of a link between the civil rights movement and international communism? Was this the bombshell the state needed to change the headlines?

On June 29, Brigadier General T. B. Birdsong— director of public safety and founder of the Mississippi Highway Patrol—called a press conference at which he promised to remove any guesswork from the assembled journalists' reporting by disclosing conclusive proof of a major communist role in planning and directing the Freedom Rides. He revealed that unnamed sources had provided unnamed state investigators with a verified list of 202 names of students who had attended a "Fair Play for Cuba" seminar in Havana the previous February. Birdsong named Kathleen Pleune of Chicago and David Wahlstorm of Madison, Wisconsin, as participants in the Cuban seminar. Both had been arrested as freedom riders in Jackson. "They're pawns in the hands of the Communists," Birdsong charged. He then went on to make a series of allegations that went far beyond the known facts. He claimed that the students had attended an intensive workshop on civil disobedience tactics con- ducted by nine agents of the Soviet Union in Cuba. He stated that the workshop had provided detailed instruc- tion on carrying out "sit-ins and walk-ins and freedom rides"—and that the Russian instructors had "inspired and directed" the entire Freedom Ride movement.

CORE immediately branded the allegations ridiculous

and the press conference an unfounded "smear tac-tic." An attorney for one of the students telegraphed Birdsong with a demand for proof that Soviet agents had led a workshop on freedom riding during the Cuban trip. Birdsong backed off. The subsequent reporting made the story relatively clear: The students had gone to Cuba with a leftist group seeking to improve Cuban-American relations, but there were no civil disobedience training sessions led by Soviet agents, and there was no tactical advice on freedom riding. The state's bid to regain the propaganda edge fizzled as the northern press lost inter-est. And more freedom riders kept coming.

Just a week later an even more insidious piece of propaganda hit the newsstands. This one came from black newsman and Commission collaborator Percy Greene. Greene's *Jackson Advocate* ran an eight-column headline above his feature story daring Reverend Martin Luther King to join a Freedom Ride to Jackson. The piece predicted that King would be arrested and would face potentially deadly consequences at Parchman. On July 6, 1961, the inflammatory article was gleefully cov-ered by the segregationist *Jackson Daily News*, which claimed that King had steered clear of the Freedom Rides because he was too busy "caddillacking around the country making speeches and taking bows."

Despite the public relations diatribes, the freedom riders continued to arrive at the depots, the police continued to make arrests, the judges continued to issue fines, and the guards kept ordering prisoners to stop singing. The scorecard of arrests and convictions that ran regularly in the *Jackson Daily News* was no longer a power statement of the state's ability to punish the "invaders." Now it was a reminder of the persistence of the protesters and the outside media attention it spawned.

As events unfolded in Jackson, Washington was applying quiet but persistent power. U.S. attorney general Robert Kennedy pushed the Interstate Commerce Commission to issue a regulation specifically barring interstate bus and rail companies from allowing segregation at their stations. Now the companies that ran the bus and train lines were subject to serious fines for allowing segregation to continue. As of September 1, 1961, the "whites only" and "Negroes only" signs at bus and rail depots gradually began to come down. The freedom riders had won a major victory, although it would take more time to fully enforce the anti-segregation law.

When it was all over, 328 riders had been arrested and jailed in Mississippi, their mug shots preserved in the files of the Commission. The mug shots of young faces—innocence mixed with fear mixed with defiance—seem frozen in time in testimony to a life-and-death struggle.

After the riders returned to their colleges in the North, it was left to local civil rights activists to contest the bus and rail stations that remained segregated. With the glare of the media gone, the local activists faced harsh and often degrading opposition.

Fannie Lou Hamer, Annelle Ponder, and June Johnson had been working on a voter registration drive in

The color line in Mississippi (exemplified by this ferry waiting room, left) was established by a complex web of laws and customs that both sides were expected to understand and adhere to. Violators could face the wrath of the state and white supremacist groups.

The roadside billboard below falsely claimed that Dr. Martin Luther King, Jr., attended a training school that taught the tenets of Communism.

MARTIN LUTHER KING AT COMMUNIST TRAINING SCHOOL

Wasting away with cancer, Clyde Kennard (below) was confined to a hospital bed after his release from the notorious Parchman prison.

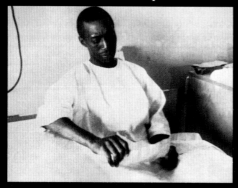

Jackson Advocate *editor Percy Greene (above) took payments in exchange for publishing propaganda and keeping tabs on civil rights leaders.*

The bus that carried freedom riders to Jackson, Mississippi (right), required heavy police and military protection.

The Sovereignty Commission kept an extensive file of mug shots of the freedom riders (a few samples below). Agents also searched their backgrounds for information that could be used to paint them as subversives.

The Commission kept photos of protest marchers in an extensive investigative file. The faces of leaders were circled in red, targeting them for further investigation – or worse.

Druggist Aaron Henry (above) served as president of the Mississippi branch of the NAACP. In retaliation for his civil rights advocacy, white opponents firebombed his store.

The FBI conducted a massive, 44-day search for civil rights activists Mickey Schwerner, Andrew Goodman, and James Chaney (right).

MISSING CALL FBI

THE FBI IS SEEKING INFORMATION CONCERNING THE DISAPPEARANCE AT PHILADELPHIA, MISSISSIPPI, OF THESE THREE INDIVIDUALS ON JUNE 21, 1964. EXTENSIVE INVESTIGATION IS BEING CONDUCTED TO LOCATE GOODMAN, CHANEY, AND SCHWERNER, WHO ARE DESCRIBED AS FOLLOWS:

ANDREW GOODMAN **JAMES EARL CHANEY** **MICHAEL HENRY SCHWERNER**

RACE:	White	Negro	White
SEX:	Male	Male	Male
DOB:	November 23, 1943	May 30, 1943	November 6, 1939
POB:	New York City	Meridian, Mississippi	New York City
AGE:	20 years	21 years	24 years
HEIGHT:	5'10"	5'7"	5'9" to 5'10"
WEIGHT:	150 pounds	135 to 140 pounds	170 to 180 pounds
HAIR:	Dark brown; wavy	Black	Brown
EYES:	Brown	Brown	Light blue
TEETH:		Good; none missing	
SCARS AND MARKS:		1 inch cut scar 2 inches above left ear.	Pock mark center of forehead, slight scar on bridge of nose, appendectomy scar, broken leg scar.

SHOULD YOU HAVE OR IN THE FUTURE RECEIVE ANY INFORMATION CONCERNING THE WHEREABOUTS OF THESE INDIVIDUALS, YOU ARE REQUESTED TO NOTIFY ME OR THE NEAREST OFFICE OF THE FBI. TELEPHONE NUMBER IS LISTED BELOW.

DIRECTOR
FEDERAL BUREAU OF INVESTIGATION
UNITED STATES DEPARTMENT OF JUSTICE
WASHINGTON, D. C. 20535
TELEPHONE, NATIONAL 8-7117

June 29, 1964

Mississippi governor Ross Barnett (above) was an avid football fan. Here white fans give him a hero's welcome.

James Meredith broke the color barrier in higher education in Mississippi.

Medgar Evers (above)—NAACP field secretary for Mississippi—was assassinated by former Klansman Byron De La Beckwith in front of his home in Jackson in June 1963. The photo at right shows where the bullet hit Evers's window after passing through his body.

Greenwood, Mississippi, when they were recruited to take
part in a workshop on freedom rider tactics in Charleston,
South Carolina. On their way home from the workshop,
their bus stopped at a Greyhound terminal café in
Winona, Mississippi. The café had a "whites only" sign
on its glass door. The newly trained African-American
freedom riders walked through the door, sat at the coun-
ter, and ordered Cokes and bags of peanuts.

The restaurant manager told them that Negroes
could only be served through the rear window and asked
them to leave. When they refused, he called the sheriff's
office. The three were promptly arrested and taken to the
county jail, where they were denied lawyers and placed
in separate cells. Then, a black female trustee—an inmate
assigned to assist the prison staff—went to Hamer's cell
and escorted her to a booking room, where the jailer was
waiting with a thick, three-inch-wide leather belt with
a handle at one end. The jailer ordered Hamer to bend
over a table and pull down her skirt. Then he handed
the belt to the trustee. A beating ensued. In short order,
Hamer and the other women were found guilty of breach
of peace, fined $100, and released.

The NAACP reported the beatings to the U.S.
Department of Justice in Washington, D.C. A week
later, Justice Department civil rights attorney St. John
Barrett interviewed the women and ordered the crime
lab to photograph their still-visible wounds. Barrett also
traveled to Mississippi with a tape recorder to interview
the jail trustee who had administered the beating. In his
personal memoir, Barrett recalls the interview:

"What were you in jail for?"

"Waiting trial on grand larceny."

"Were you a trustee?"

"Yes, sir."

"What does that mean?"

"That means they trusted me. They would let me out of my cell to do the jobs around the jail, like mopping the floors, peeling potatoes, washing dishes, taking meals to the cells—stuff like that."

"Did the jailer have a strap?"

"Yes, sir."

"Did you ever use the strap?"

"Yes, sir. He had me use it on the prisoners who broke the rules. But I only used it when he ordered me to and only for the number of pops he ordered."

"When the two women were brought to the jail, were you in your cell?"

"No, sir. I was mopping the floor."

"Tell me what happened."

"Well, the police and the jailer put the women in separate cells in the women's section. They didn't book or fingerprint them. The police talked for a while and then the jailer told me to get the heavier woman out of her cell and bring her to the booking room. When I brought her, he told her to take her skirt down and lay on a table on her stomach. She didn't say anything and did like he said. The jailer handed me the strap and told me to give her a few good licks. I gave her a few and he told me to hit her harder and don't stop until he told me to. I kept on going until I saw she was bleeding. I looked at the jailer and he said O.K."

11

THE BATTLE
FOR OLE MISS

Clyde Kennard had been denied a college education and railroaded into prison, but the dream of breaking the color barrier in higher education in Mississippi lived on. The next attempt came from James Howard Meredith, a Mississippi native, U.S. Air Force veteran, and Jackson State College student. Meredith was also a very private person and an intense proponent of racial equality. He was a man with a mission.

Meredith seemed destined to challenge the racial status quo from as far back as his childhood in poverty-racked Attala County. His father, Cap, was the son of a former slave who had worked tirelessly to acquire his own land and register to vote. Cap built a fence around his family farm to keep trouble out and taught his son J. H. never to abide by the custom of entering a white person's house only through the back door.

In the air force, J. H. was stationed in Japan, where he was deeply moved by the Japanese people's acceptance of blacks. Meredith went home with a strong desire to help his own country become more tolerant. Encouraged by the election of President Kennedy and the integration of several segregated southern colleges and universities, he began to envision himself breaking the color barrier in Mississippi.

An outstanding student at all-black Jackson State, Meredith applied to transfer to the prestigious University of Mississippi—one of the state's most prominent symbols of white privilege and power. Located in the quaint town of Oxford and steeped in the traditions of the Old South, Ole Miss was the school of choice for the children of Mississippi's white elite. On February 4, 1961, Meredith received a telegram from the Ole Miss admissions officer denying his application. Three days later the Ole Miss Board of Trustees voted to revise the admission rules to give the school even more leeway to deny him—or any applicant—from entering. The NAACP filed a lawsuit on Meredith's behalf, claiming that he had been denied admission because of his race. The state courts backed the trustees with the dubious ruling that there was no official policy of segregation at Ole Miss, even if no black student had ever been enrolled there.

As the case moved through the courts, the Sovereignty Commission sent investigators Andy Hopkins and Virgil Downing to Attala County to investigate Meredith's relationship with his parents. After arriving in the hardscrabble farming community, the agents stopped at the county courthouse to pore through public records and interviewed county officials and local police to learn more about the Merediths. The investigation turned up nothing that would sink James's application. The records showed he had purchased 84 acres from his father in 1960 and had secured license

plates for a 1959 Volkswagen and a 1952 Cadillac.
Sheriff W. T. Wasson told the agents that he had "known
Cap Meredith for 20 years and that he knew him to
be a good colored person." The black superintendent
of the Coahoma County Separate School District,
J. T. Coleman, told investigators that James Meredith's
mother, Roxie, worked for $14 a week as a cook in the
Tipton Street School. Unsolicited, Coleman threatened to
fire Roxie if she ever publicly supported her son's aspira-
tion to attend Ole Miss. "Mr. Coleman also stated that
should the schools in Mississippi ever be integrated, the
schools would be ruined," Downing reported, "and that
he would do everything he possibly could to keep the
schools segregated."

The agents concluded that Cap and Roxie Meredith
were determined to maintain a low profile. They hoped
their neighbors would not link them to the man behind
the Ole Miss controversy, which had become front-page
news even in rural backwaters like Attala County. The
agents also knew how to let the entire county know that
the "integration agitator" at Ole Miss had roots in their
community. Cap and Roxie's low profile was shattered
when the investigative report was leaked to the Jackson
Clarion Ledger. On June 16, 1961, the paper ran a local
story headlined "Meredith Drives Cadillac and Compact
to Visit Pop." But the spies' small-town maneuverings
would soon be eclipsed by stunning national news.

June 25, 1962, was James Meredith's 29th birthday.
It was also the day a federal appeals court sent shivers

down the spine of the entire white power structure in Mississippi. The Fifth Circuit Court of Appeals overturned the state court ruling and found that Meredith had been denied entry solely because of his race, victimized by "a carefully calculated campaign of delay, harassment, and masterful inactivity." The court ordered that Meredith be admitted that September. The order set the stage for a dramatic showdown between Governor Barnett and President Kennedy aided by his brother, Attorney General Robert Kennedy. The clock was ticking. The start of the fall semester was just a few months away.

In July, the Sovereignty Commission rushed Hopkins and Downing back to Attala County in a desperate effort to unearth damaging information on the Merediths. The investigations again proved fruitless.

As fall approached, Commission public relations director Erle Johnston rushed an order to the printer for more than a million postcards with a preprinted message expressing resentment at the "unnatural warfare being waged against the sovereign state of Mississippi." The cards—to be signed by white voters throughout the South—were addressed to President Kennedy, White House, Washington, D.C.

On the evening of September 13, Governor Barnett went on statewide television and declared the standoff to be "our greatest crisis since the War Between the States" and pledging to resist "the evil and illegal forces of tyranny." Repeating his promise that "no school will be integrated while I am your governor," Barnett asked for the resignation of any state official unwilling to "suffer imprisonment for this righteous cause."

On the afternoon of September 20, Barnett entered
a boardroom on the Ole Miss campus, ready for the
first of what would prove to be several dramatic face-
to-face confrontations with federal marshals who had
been assigned to escort Meredith to register for the fall
semester. The governor read a statement denying the
application, and the marshals and Meredith walked away
to try again another day. In a similar confrontation on
September 25, Barnett pulled out his trademark humor
to endear himself to his supporters and to frustrate his
foes. Surrounded by his white supporters as a phalanx
of white federal marshals led Meredith into the room,
Barnett looked into the sea of white faces and asked,
"Which one of you is Mr. Meredith?" The federal agents
scowled, Meredith smiled, and the onlookers howled.

As events continued to unfold, Barnett was buying
time by carrying on secret phone conversations with
President Kennedy and Attorney General Kennedy,
who were now committed to enforcing the court order
despite the probable loss of support from powerful
southerners in Congress. The governor tried unsuccessfully to convince the Kennedy brothers to postpone
the enrollment indefinitely, warning that bloody riots
would shake the campus if a black student were allowed
to enroll.

Barnett, needing a point man for the delicate negotiations with the Kennedys, turned to his close friend and
confidant Tom Watkins, a successful private attorney
and member of the governing board of the Sovereignty

Commission. Manning the phone line to Washington, Watkins became the key conduit between Barnett and the two Kennedys.

With all sides grappling for a solution, Watkins proposed a series of schemes designed to get Meredith safely ensconced at Ole Miss and to allow Barnett to save his reputation as a staunch, unbending segregationist. Watkins warned that "if there is to be any school integration in Mississippi, it would have to be done forcefully." In one carefully orchestrated scheme, a federal marshal was to shove Barnett aside and move past him to register the student. Feigning shock, Barnett would save face by condemning the use of federal force against a sitting governor. The stage was set, the actors had their roles, and the curtain was rising when the script abruptly changed: Barnett's plane was grounded by bad weather in Jackson and Lieutenant Governor Paul Johnson was left to take his place in Oxford. Unfortunately, no one had shared the script with Johnson, who refused to stand aside and pushed back hard against the dumbfounded marshal. The defiant act ingratiated Johnson with the white masses and proved invaluable to his future political career.

Another plan called for the governor and his supporters to make a historic last stand at a gate to Ole Miss, face-to-face with 30 armed federal marshals acting as a shield for Meredith. The lead marshal would pull his gun and point it at Barnett, who would only then call upon his supporters to stand down to avoid bloodshed. When Robert Kennedy repeated the scheme to Barnett and Watkins over the phone, the governor demurred. He would only sound the retreat if all 30 marshals pulled their weapons and threatened to fire.

"I was under the impression that they were all going to pull their guns," Barnett told an exasperated Robert Kennedy. "If one pulls his gun and we all turn, it would be very embarrassing."

Then the secret phone negotiations took a bizarre twist. Faced with a federal contempt-of-court charge, a $10,000-per-day fine, and possible jail time, the savior of segregation began to cave to the pressure of pending financial ruin and imprisonment. His hundreds of thousands of white supporters would have been horrified to learn that the chief executive of their "sovereign" state was secretly working with the "forces of tyranny" to assure a black man's peaceful enrollment at Ole Miss—this from the man who had publicly proclaimed, "Ross Barnett will rot in a federal jail before he lets one nigra cross the threshold of our sacred white schools." The enemies of segregation were closing in, and Barnett was now negotiating the terms of surrender.

On Saturday, September 29, President Kennedy himself called Barnett to offer a new plan. It called for the governor to rally his forces at the Oxford campus while federal marshals quietly registered Meredith at a state college board office in Jackson. The date was set for Monday, October 1. Barnett could save face by accusing the Kennedys of registering the black student behind his back. Barnett and Watkins agreed to the plan and promised to use the Mississippi Highway Patrol and Mississippi National Guard to maintain calm at Ole Miss. It turns out that both the Kennedy brothers and

Barnett were football fans and, in the parlance of the game, their plan resembled a hidden ball trick, in which a running back pretends to have the ball while the actual ball carrier, unnoticed, carries it downfield.

So there was some irony that the big football game between Ole Miss and Kentucky was scheduled for Jackson's Memorial Stadium that very night. At game time, more than 46,000 fans packed the stands, where the Meredith showdown was generating more buzz than the game itself. As Barnett walked to the governor's box, the crowd began waving Confederate flags and chanting, "We want Ross. We want Ross." Barnett, the consummate political showman, couldn't resist the adoration. Despite his promise to the Kennedys to maintain calm, he chose to play the hero one more time. At halftime he walked to midfield, stood at a microphone, clenched his fist, waved his arms, and shouted, "I love Mississippi, I love her people. I love our customs." The crowd went into a frenzy.

Ole Miss student Gerald Blessy recalled the scene years later: "I looked back at the crowd and saw anger in the faces of the people right next to me and it sort of flashed through my mind that those rebel flags looked liked swastikas. These were just ordinary school kids who were being whipped into a fever pitch of emotion by their own leaders. It was just like the Nazis had done."

Commission public relations chief Erle Johnston had a different recollection of Barnett's speech: "As he stood there, smiling, acknowledging the cheers of the multitude, he was more than a governor of Mississippi. He was a symbol of the South, with the red blood of his Confederate soldier father running through his veins."

After the game hundreds of students began the 175-mile drive to Oxford. They were spoiling for a fight. And Barnett called Washington and left a message for Robert Kennedy: The deal to enroll Meredith was off. In the game to come, there would be no hidden ball trick.

The next morning, Sunday, September 30, an infuriated attorney general called Barnett with a threat. The President was prepared to go on national television that night to tell the American people that "you had an agreement to permit Meredith to go to Jackson to register, and your lawyer, Mr. Watkins, said this was satisfactory." Barnett's blood ran cold. This would mean that the entire nation would know of his secret talk with the Kennedys. Even more important, the entire white power structure of the state of Mississippi would know that the ardent segregationist and former Klansman had sold out the cause. The official transcript of the phone conversation reads as follows:

RB [Ross Barnett]: *That won't do at all.*
RFK [Robert Kennedy]: *You broke your word to him.*
RB: *You don't mean the President is going to say that tonight?*
RFK: *Of course he is; you broke your word; now you suggest we send in troops, fighting their way through a barricade. You gave your word. Mr. Watkins gave him his word. You didn't keep it.*
RB: *Don't say that. Please don't mention it.*

The Attorney General then instructed Barnett and Watkins to prepare a statement to be read by the governor on statewide TV that night. They would consent to the enrollment and call for calm at Ole Miss. Barnett and Watkins wrote a script and reviewed it with Robert Kennedy later that day. The pillar of segregated education in Mississippi would fall to the earth with these words by Ross Barnett: "My heart says never but my good judgment abhors the bloodshed that would follow. . . . We must at all odds preserve the peace and avoid bloodshed."

Despite the capitulation, President Kennedy had given up on Barnett. Forget the hidden ball trick. The President was charging through Barnett's front line. He placed the Mississippi National Guard under his authority and alerted the U.S. Army base at Memphis to prepare for possible deployment to Oxford. As the military units moved into action that eventful Sunday, student mobs began roaming the campus, shouting racial slurs and hurling rocks and bricks. Hundreds of armed men—including Klansmen from across the South and white militias from as far away as California—began arriving in Oxford to take on the federal forces. At about 5:30 p.m., Meredith was escorted to the Ole Miss campus by dozens of U.S. marshals wearing gas masks, vests, and helmets and equipped with tear-gas launchers, batons, and sidearms. Within an hour, Ole Miss erupted into a full-scale riot. For hours, clouds of tear gas rode the breeze, and the sound of gunshots crackled in the night. Mississippi National Guard troops arrived at about 11 p.m., and U.S. Army units showed up at 2 a.m. By the end of the long night, more than 20,000 troops had descended on the campus. They seized control, restored order, and arrested more than 200 people. Two people were dead, and 165 federal agents were injured—23 by gunfire. On Monday, October 1, 1962, James H. Meredith attended his first class. The subject was American history.

In a telling footnote, six weeks later Commission investigator Tom Scarborough went to Attala County to continue the investigation into Meredith's parents. Scarborough reported that Cap and Roxie had refused an appeal from Sheriff Wasson to go with him to Jackson to persuade their son to drop out of Ole Miss or—short of that—to speak out against his enrollment in the newspapers. The elder Merediths wanted nothing to do with the controversy, insisting that James rarely visited them and never discussed his role at Ole Miss.

Still, the agent couldn't resist reporting his personal conclusion: "It is my opinion that both mama and papa Meredith are not opposed to what their now-famous son had done and is doing. To the contrary they are proud of what James Meredith has done by entering the University of Mississippi and bringing about riots, strife, turmoil, and even death."

CHAPTER 12

IN THE DEAD OF THE NIGHT

The time:	*Just after midnight*
The date:	*June 12, 1963*
The place:	*A quiet, moonlit, suburban street on the outskirts of Jackson*
The threat:	*A lone gunman crouching behind a clump of honeysuckle vines*
The target:	*NAACP state field secretary Medgar Evers*

The gunman lifts the thirty-ought-six, high-powered Enfield hunting rifle to his shoulder and places a squinting eye to its six-power telescopic sight. Evers pulls his blue 1962 Oldsmobile into the driveway of the ranch-style house at 2332 Guyness Street. He opens the car door and steps out. He holds a stack of T-shirts emblazed with the slogan "Jim Crow Must Go." The events of the next hour will change history.

On that fateful night, Evers was returning home from an evening of NAACP functions. He had updated his colleagues on the protest demonstrations shaking the state's capital and had watched President Kennedy make a televised address, announcing plans to push new civil rights legislation in Congress and urging citizens to embrace tolerance and understanding over prejudice and hatred.

For his part, Evers had been prodding his NAACP colleagues to move beyond their courtroom arguments and economic boycotts to embrace the new, direct-action protests employed by student activists. His embrace of those tactics had led to a series of student marches and sit-ins in Jackson that spring, which had spurred more than 700 arrests and had generated intense media coverage. Once dubbed a "quiet integrationist" by the *New York Times,* Evers was now being called a dangerous radical by the segregationist press at home. His high profile was also prompting hate mail, death threats, and attempts on his life. In a two-week period in late May and early June 1963, a Molotov cocktail had been thrown into his carport and a speeding car had nearly run him down outside his office in Jackson.

Despite the dangers, Evers pressed forward. The principle of doing the right thing in the face of hardship had been impressed upon him by his parents during his childhood in the mill town of Decatur, Mississippi, in the 1920s and 1930s. The hardships of life in a small, segregated town had included the day-to-day indignities of second-class citizenship and the hoots and howls of gangs of white hooligans, who roamed the streets on weekends and tossed firecrackers at black children. Evers dropped out of school in the 11th grade to join the army and fight in World War II. On the battlefields of Europe he waged war on the Nazis—the ultimate white supremacists—and learned that the defense of freedom carried the risk of death. Off the battlefields in Europe, he dated a white woman and discovered that racial segregation was not a universal reality. After returning home to Decatur, he tried to register to vote, only to be roughed up by a white mob. He vowed to make a difference.

Evers finished high school and earned a degree in business administration at Alcorn A & M College. Setting out to prove that an African American could succeed in the Deep South, Evers took a job selling insurance for the black-owned Magnolia Mutual Life Insurance Company. Realizing the futility of pedaling life-insurance policies to poor black dirt farmers who could barely afford food and shelter for their families, he put away the insurance policies and began handing out application forms for the NAACP. In the early 1950s, he started writing reports for the organization, chronicling the deplorable state of Negro schools and the prevalence of Klan violence. In 1954 he was named the organization's first Mississippi field secretary. In that role, he logged thousands of miles driving the state's two-lane highways and two-rut dirt roads as he investigated lynchings, voter intimidation, and police brutality.

Naturally, Evers had long been a subject of keen interest to the Commission. In the field secretary's first years on the job, special operative T1 launched a basic background check on him, and agent Van Landingham tracked his movements. Van Landingham seriously underestimated the quiet and introspective activist. He filed a report that predicted Evers would fail to connect with grassroots activists because "he is a weak character and a coward" afraid to put himself "at forefront or in a position that would place him in danger of bodily harm." Before long the opinionated investigator was compiling extensive, 6- to 12-page memos on Evers's relentless activism as he built a dossier under the subject heading "Medgar Evers: Integration Agitator." The file included Evers's military records, college transcripts, car registration, and the birth certificates of his children.

Van Landingham also chronicled Evers's attacks on the Commission. In a report on an NAACP meeting, he noted, "Evers spoke regarding the State Sovereignty Commission and mentioned my name as receiving reports from Negro informants all over the state."

In fact, the Commission's confidential informants had tracked the field secretary's movements for years. And working in tandem with the Jackson City Police, they were closely monitoring his actions that spring of 1963, as picket lines and sit-ins disrupted the daily flow of events in the state's capital.

In May 1963 Commission agents intercepted a letter that Evers wrote to supporters and placed it in his investigative file. "The NAACP is determined to put an end to all forms of radical segregation in Jackson," Evers wrote. "To accomplish this we shall use all lawful means of protests—picketing, marches, mass mailings, litigation, and whatever other lawful means we deem necessary."

At another point Evers directly challenged the white power structure by going over the heads of all state officials to appeal to ordinary citizens: "We believe that there are white Mississippians who want to go forward on the race question. Their religion tells them there is something wrong with the old system. Their sense of justice and fair play sends them the same message. But whether Jackson and the state choose to change or not, the years of change are upon us."

Things never would be the same after June 12, 1963. Just after midnight, Evers stepped out of the car with the bundle of "Jim Crow Must Go" T-shirts and walked up his driveway with his door key in hand. His wife, Myrlie, was watching television in the bedroom with their three children nestled on the bed with her. As Medgar Evers walked toward the front door, the gunman in the shadows squeezed the trigger. The shot rang out, breaking the silence. The bullet ripped through Evers's back below his right shoulder blade, through a window, and through a wall inside the house. As Evers crawled to his front porch with blood pouring from his body and his keys still in hand, Myrlie ran out, horrified. Their children had taken cover under the bed as their parents had taught them to do at the sound of gunshots. They ran out a few minutes later to see their father lying in a pool of blood. Myrlie rushed back inside and called the police. Her husband was rushed to the hospital but died 50 minutes later.

The next morning Jackson City Police scoured the crime scene. Detective Sergeant O. M. Luke found the thirty-ought-six rifle in a honeysuckle vine less than 400 feet from Evers's driveway. Jackson Police Captain Ralph Hargrove photographed the scene and took the rifle back to his office to examine. As he meticulously dusted the rifle for prints, a single index finger print on the scope "practically jumped up." Hargrove sent the print to the FBI, which matched it with a print in a military file belonging to Byron De La Beckwith, a founding member of the White Citizens' Council and a Klansman from Greenville. It turned out that De La Beckwith also drove a white Plymouth Valiant, the same color and make of car seen prowling Evers's neighborhood the day of the murder.

De La Beckwith was not completely unknown to the Commission. Deep in its secret files was a letter he had written in 1957 to then-governor Coleman asking for a job with the segregation watchdogs. In the letter, De La Beckwith listed his qualifications: "Expert with a pistol, good with a rifle and fair with a shotgun—and—RABID ON THE SUBJECT OF SEGREGATION! I therefore request that you select me, among many, as one who will tear the mask from the face of the NAACP and forever rid this fair land of the DISEASE OF INTEGRATION with which it is plagued with." He wasn't hired.

As the civil rights community mourned, tragedy struck again. An outcry was building in the North over the worsening condition of Clyde Kennard, still serving a seven-year sentence at Parchman on trumped-up charges of being an accomplice to theft of five bags of chicken feed. With cancer ravishing Kennard's body, Barnett finally granted him clemency to avoid the public relations nightmare of allowing a political prisoner to die in custody. Two months after returning to Chicago, on the Fourth of July of 1963, Clyde Kennard died of cancer. Ironically, Evers had spoken out on Kennard's behalf for years and had even been held in comtempt of court for decrying Kennard's sentence. Now both men were gone.

Amid the gloom, the state came under intense pressure to bring Evers's killer to justice. In late June, De La Beckwith was arrested and charged with murder. Under police questioning, De La Beckwith claimed that his rifle had been stolen before the shooting. He also claimed that he was playing cards with friends on the night of the murder. Two of those friends turned out to be police officers, and they backed up his alibi in court. During the high-profile trial, the defendant—clad in a linen suit, monogrammed shirt, and French cuffs—appeared cocky and unrepentant. During breaks in the proceedings, he strutted around the courtroom, offered cigars to the prosecutor, chatted cotton prices with farmers in the gallery, and whispered racist quotes to reporters. As the White Citizens' Council raised funds for his defense, De La Beckwith became a poster boy for racial hatred. In the end, the all-white jury could not agree upon a verdict, and a mistrial was declared.

Certain that De La Beckwith was guilty, state prosecutors prepared for a retrial. The De La Beckwith defense team knew that its best hope was to seat another

jury incapable of reaching a unanimous guilty verdict.
Another hung jury would force the court to set De La
Beckwith free. At that point defense attorney Stanney
Sanders called Commission investigator Andy Hopkins
with a highly unusual request. He asked Hopkins to
screen 11 prospective jurors for the defense. Hopkins,
an FBI-trained investigator, was uneasy. He questioned
the ethics of intervening on behalf of the defense in
the state prosecution of a high-profile murder case.
He asked his Commission superiors for permission to
intervene and got the go-ahead. The only caveat: Avoid
direct, personal contact with prospective jurors.

Hopkins called the prospective jurors' employers and
associates and compiled a report on their work histories
and affiliations, including their involvement in groups
like the White Citizens' Council. Next to one man's
name the agent scrawled "believed to be Jewish" (that
prospective juror was dismissed), and next to others he
wrote "fair and impartial" (those jurors were seated). In
the end, the all-white, all-male, all-Protestant jury dead-
locked, and De La Beckwith went free—to brag at Klan
rallies of getting away with murder. Given his ability
to postpone justice, he was tagged with the nickname
Delay Beckwith.

THE SECRET BENEFACTOR

Who: *President John F. Kennedy*

What: *A sweeping civil rights bill under debate in Congress. The measure would outlaw segregation in public places, including schools, government buildings, parks, retail stores, restaurants, and theaters.*

When: *Early 1963*

Where: *Washington, D.C.*

Why: *In Kennedy's own words, "A great change is at hand, and our task, our obligation, is to make that revolution, that change, peaceful and constructive for all. Those who do nothing are inviting shame, as well as violence. Those who act boldly are recognizing right, as well as reality."*

As the President pressed members of Congress to support the groundbreaking legislation, southern Democrats and conservative Republicans dug in their heels and braced for a fight. Key opponents of the bill also formed a well-financed and highly organized lobbying group to wage a political and public relations war

against the Kennedy civil rights program. Few observ-
ers on the national political scene realized that the anti–
civil rights lobbying campaign was—in large part—being
funded and organized by a secretive state agency in
far-off Mississippi. The Commission had gone national.

Public relations chief Erle Johnston had been pro-
moted to director of the Commission and was demon-
strating a knack for high-level political maneuvering.
In summer of 1963, Johnston traveled to Washington,
D.C., to take part in a hush-hush conference "to lay
plans for an organized effort to defeat the new Kennedy
civil rights program." In the weeks to come, Johnston,
Sovereignty Commission attorney John Satterfield, and
several prominent conservative political leaders formed
the Coordinating Committee for Fundamental American
Freedoms, a national lobbying organization dedicated
to defeating the Kennedy bill. Operating from a plush
suite of offices overlooking congressional staff buildings on Capitol Hill, the group pumped out speeches,
press releases, and newspaper ads denouncing the bill,
falsely claiming it would require employers to replace
white workers with black workers, destroy the national
budget, and lead to socialism. The campaign became the
most costly lobbying effort of its day.

The lobbying program was funded primarily by the
Commission, which had raised private donations in
Mississippi and had tapped its own budget to jump-start
the effort. In addition, it had taken in $209,010 in pri-
vate donations (more than $1.8 million in today's money)
from a single, anonymous, out-of-state donor.

The secret benefactor was a wealthy white

supremacist from New York named Wickliffe Preston
Draper, who had funded social experiments aimed at
breeding a white superrace and research into the pros-
pects of resettling blacks in Africa. How frightening
were Draper and his associates? Prior to World War II,
Draper attended a conference in Berlin and befriended
German interior minister Wilhelm Frick, who ended
up being hanged for crimes against humanity after the
war. At the conference, Draper's travel companion and
colleague Dr. Clarence Campbell sympathized with the
Germans on the issue of race and ethnicity. "The differ-
ences between the Jew and the Aryan," he said, "are as
insurmountable as that between black and white."

During the legislative battle over the Kennedy bill,
Draper's financial support was kept under wraps. As far
as the segregationists were concerned, the public had
no need to know that the anti–civil rights lobby was
being bankrolled by a white supremacist and Nazi sympathizer and that his money had been routed through
a segregationist spy agency to the lobbying campaign.
Then came the shocking assassination of President
Kennedy in Dallas on November 22, 1963. Would this
end the push for a new civil rights bill? The answer
turned out to be no. Five days after the assassination,
President Johnson urged a joint session of Congress
to pay homage to the fallen leader by passing the Civil
Rights Act of 1964. The legislative battle raged on.

CHAPTER

AGENT X

A tall, well-dressed black man strides with confidence down the hallway of the Masonic Temple in the heart of the bustling "colored section" of Jackson, Mississippi, in March 1964. He stops at a door leading to the large meeting room, waits for a nod from a man standing guard, and takes a seat in the spectators' gallery. Scanning the faces of the men and women sitting at the meeting table in the center of the room, he recognizes a virtual who's who of the state's civil rights leadership, including the highest-ranking leaders of the NAACP and SNCC. The unassuming spectator listens intently. No one in the room suspects that the seemingly innocuous visitor has his own agenda. Far from being a sympathizer with the cause, he is actually a private detective being paid to keep tabs on the civil rights crusaders for the segregationist state.

After the meeting, the private eye reports to his superiors at the Day Detective Agency in Jackson. He provides a synopsis of the meeting and a document marked "Confidential: Mississippi Freedom Summer." The Day detectives will supply a full report to their prized client, the Mississippi State Sovereignty Commission. The report—single-spaced on plain white paper—will bear the telltale mark of a hand-scrawled X with a circle around it—the sign that it originated with a top secret, black informant code-named Agent X.

The report from Agent X described plans for an extensive voter registration campaign to be carried out across the state over the coming summer. The project would link hundreds—perhaps even thousands—of mostly white college students from the North with dozens of black freedom workers from Mississippi. Three major civil rights organizations—the NAACP, SNCC, and CORE—would execute the campaign under the umbrella of the Council of Federated Organizations (COFO).

The document attached to the report said that more than 2,000 students, teachers, nurses, and legal advisers would form a "Peace Corps–type operation" designed to transform race relations in the state. The volunteers would set up Freedom Schools to teach reading and writing to black children and teens and establish community centers to provide adult literacy classes and vocational training programs to adults. Volunteers would also prepare thousands of blacks to register to vote for the first time and lay the groundwork for black candidates to run for public office.

"The program of voter registration and political organization will attempt to change the fundamental structure of political and economic activity in Mississippi," the report stated.

As plans for Freedom Summer developed, Agent X

continued to feed intelligence to the Commission, revealing the organizers' plans to prepare "Negros to run for the United States Congress." "It appears now that one of the main purposes of the proposed statewide voter registration campaign is directed to this end," one of Agent X's reports stated. The infiltrator considered no piece of intelligence insignificant. He even reported plans for a "completely integrated" folk concert starring singer Joan Baez on April 5, 1964, at Tougaloo College to drum up interest in the summer offensive.

As Freedom Summer grew closer, Agent X struck again. He persuaded the COFO leadership to put him on the staff. "After a few interviews," he reported to the commission, "I was offered a position." Upon gaining the trust of the COFO staff, the spy began searching the office for confidential reports that would reveal the latest plans. The clever infiltrator patiently awaited his chance to intercept the documents. On June 2, he told his handlers, "I decided it would be better to wait another day before picking up this literature."

At an opportune moment, Agent X secretly copied the applications of student activists accepted into the Freedom Summer program. He passed the names, addresses, driver's license numbers, and photographs on to the Commission.

As the clock continued to tick, Agent X wrangled an invitation to an extensive training seminar for several hundred student activists to be held at the Western College for Women in Oxford, Ohio, on June 16, 1964. On that date, Director Johnston was informed that "X is departing this date for Oxford, Ohio, with wife and will forward reports to a blind P.O. Box here in Jackson and make periodic telephone reports on activities."

Upon arriving on the campus on June 17, X seamlessly blended in to sessions preparing the student activists for the danger ahead. Posing as one of the few black activists from Mississippi, he gained access to sessions on registering voters, dealing with police brutality, and opening the Freedom Schools.

During one session his friend R. Jess Brown, a black lawyer from Jackson, told the students, "Now get this in your heads and remember what I am going to say. They—the white folk, the police, the state police—they are all waiting for you. They are looking for you. They are ready. They are armed. They know some of your names and your descriptions even now, even before you get to Mississippi."

Naturally, Agent X knew that all too well. He was one of the secret operatives making sure that the state was fully prepared. He and his confederates had supplied the Commission with extensive information on Freedom Summer throughout that spring and had filed more extensive reports through his 11 days at the training seminar. He revealed the names, descriptions, and destinations of key activists; the role to be played by volunteer lawyers; the plans of key reporters covering the initiative; and the mounting fears of students destined for hostile territory.

As X fed the pipeline, the Commission staff worked diligently to prepare the state to repel the invaders.

Commission agent Tom Scarborough set up meetings
across the state to prepare public officials and civic
leaders for the onslaught of northern college students.
"The purpose of these meetings has been to organize
the city and county officials to work in a coordinated
unit to handle the racial agitators who have promised to
invade Mississippi this summer," Scarborough reported.
In Lafayette County, Scarborough warned community
leaders that the invasion would be led by "communists,
sex perverts, odd balls, and do-gooders." Meeting with
a group of newly elected county sheriffs, Scarborough
warned the incoming lawmen that many of their counties were destined to be overrun by radicals. The law
enforcement community was getting edgy.

Commission agents also set out to visit sheriff's
offices in all 82 counties to prepare law enforcement
officers for potential trouble. The agents provided police
with a summary of 19 state laws that could be used
to arrest or detain troublemakers. Their goal was to
strengthen the hand of county sheriff's offices statewide,
which had been fortified with hundreds of newly deputized auxiliary officers. The police were gearing up for a
virtual war with the "outside agitators."

As the Commission fueled the fevered preparations, a
new development arose. Agent Andy Hopkins had been
investigating the intense competition for recruits between violent new factions of the Klan. One night shots
were fired into Hopkins's house, and Klan literature was
left in his yard. It appeared that the resurgent Klan was

gearing up for war, too. The new Klan was so extreme that it was ready to take on the Commission itself—on top of their common enemy—in defense of white rule.

The wild swirl of events was cascading out of the control of a state leadership that had changed dramatically over the past six months. Former lieutenant governor Paul Johnson had been elected to succeed his mentor Ross Barnett after running on the slogan "Stand Tall with Paul," reminding voters of his stand in the schoolhouse door at Ole Miss. Commission director Erle Johnston was advising the new governor on the state's preparations for Freedom Summer. But as the summer program drew close, Johnston informed his boss of "secret organizations of white people, whose mission apparently is to take laws into their own hands."

In fact, the newly formed and violent White Knights of the Ku Klux Klan were entering dozens of recruits in the newly formed auxiliary police units. These Klansmen would not wear hoods and robes to confront the "invaders"; instead, they would wear badges and carry state-issued firearms. As Freedom Summer approached, the imperial wizard of the White Knights, Sam Bowers, told his followers, "The first contact with the troops of the enemy in the street should be as legally deputized law enforcement officers."

CHAPTER 15

MARKED MEN

Michael Schwerner, Andrew Goodman, and James Chaney were at the Freedom Summer training seminar in Ohio, too. As the three young activists listened to lectures, attended workshops, and sang freedom songs, they never imagined that a black segregationist spy was watching, listening, and reporting back to Mississippi. On June 20, 1964, the three climbed into their CORE-issued, blue 1963 Ford Fairlane station wagon and set out for the Magnolia State. The ultimate destination was Mt. Zion Methodist Church in Neshoba County, Mississippi. Three nights earlier, Klansmen had doused the church with kerosene and set it ablaze. The activists wanted to help the congregation rebuild the church to make good on plans to use it as a Freedom School.

Like many of the Freedom Summer volunteers, Schwerner, Goodman, and Chaney were in their 20s, idealistic, and committed, but they hailed from vastly different backgrounds.

Michael "Mickey" Schwerner was 24, white, college educated, and married. He was the son of a successful businessman and a high school biology teacher from New York. Mickey sported a trademark goatee and loved sports, rock music, poker, and comedian W. C. Fields. In his application to serve as a CORE organizer, Schwerner vowed to spend the rest of his life working toward an integrated society. He had spent the previous summer registering voters in Meridian, Mississippi.

Andrew Goodman was a 20-year-old white graduate of a liberal, private high school in New York, who had gone on to study at Queens College. He hailed from an affluent, politically connected family that owned a share of the left-leaning Pacifica radio network. Goodman had a flair for music and acting. He felt that a summer of civil rights work in Mississippi would extend his horizons beyond his privileged background.

James Chaney was a 21-year-old, poor, black native of Meridian, Mississippi. His mother cleaned houses for white families, and his father had worked construction jobs as a plasterer before he had left the family. As Chaney matured, he recognized the depth of discrimination in his hometown and saw civil rights work as a route out.

On the afternoon of June 21, 1964, Schwerner, Goodman, and Chaney rolled in to Neshoba County en route to the ruins of the Mt. Zion Methodist Church. Chaney was at the wheel of the station wagon, license number H 25503. The car was already on a watch list at the Neshoba County sheriff's office. In the wild swirl of events leading up to Freedom Summer, the Commission had sent the information to law enforcement officials across the state, and the White Citizens' Council had picked it up and circulated it as well. Schwerner was particularly well known to the authorities, given his work registering voters in Meridian the year before. Schwerner was also well known to the White Knights of the Ku Klux Klan, whose leaders nicknamed him Goatee and targeted him for death.

At about 4 p.m., Neshoba County deputy sheriff Cecil Price pulled over the car. Price arrested Chaney for speeding and took all three men to the jail in nearby Philadelphia. As the men sat in their cells, armed Klansmen began gathering outside. At about 10:30 p.m., the police released the three, with the Klansmen still milling on the street. As the activists climbed back into their car and headed out of town, Deputy Price followed in a squad car. The Klansmen were close behind.

The next day the activists' burned-out station wagon was found in the Bogue Chitto Swamp outside Philadelphia. There was no sign of the three men. Their disappearance spurred an international media frenzy and a massive search. Even President Johnson got involved, consoling the activists' families and order-ing FBI director J. Edgar Hoover to lead the search. The President also ordered Hoover to take down the Mississippi Klan—once and for all.

Naturally, the Commission had the situation covered on all sides. Just before his departure from the Ohio train-ing seminar, Agent X had reported that student activists had gotten word of the disappearances and were being flooded with phone calls and telegrams from relatives urging them to withdraw from the project. Commission agent Andy Hopkins had rushed to Philadelphia to monitor events and to shadow the FBI. A former FBI man himself, Hopkins reported that the town was abuzz with rumors that "these subjects met with foul play either while in custody of the sheriff or shortly after their release."

A few days later Hopkins reported more talk around town: "There are rumors that there is a KKK in Philadelphia and some prominent citizens are members of the Klan." Despite the talk, Hopkins maintained the view of many locals, who insisted the incident was a publicity stunt designed to grab headlines. Hopkins also complained that FBI agents were elbowing state investigators out of the probe and strong-arming suspects for information. A couple weeks into the investigation, however, Hopkins conceded that the FBI tactics were getting results—particularly their round-the-clock surveillance of suspected Klansmen and their willingness to dole out tens of thousands of dollars for information.

The search for the missing men went on for six weeks. The FBI dragged swamps and searched woods. The Mississippi Highway Patrol kept watch across the state in the event that the missing men showed up unexpectedly. The Jackson *Clarion Ledger* speculated that the three "agitators" were probably in "Cuba or another Communist area awaiting their next task." Then the speculation ended. On August 4, 1964, 44 days after the civil rights workers were last seen alive, FBI agents dug up their bodies, buried deep into an earthen dam on a secluded farm outside Philadelphia. Commission agent Hopkins supplied his bosses with a hand-drawn map showing the burial site, noting that the bodies were discovered 14 feet down.

The tragic discovery put a worldwide spotlight on Klan violence in Mississippi. But as the headlines and television reports circled the globe, the violence and reprisals against civil rights advocates continued in the Magnolia State. Over the course of the summer, more than 40 black churches were burned and hundreds of activists were jailed. For their part, the Freedom Summer volunteers registered 1,600 new black voters, opened 37 Freedom Schools, and organized a biracial slate of candidates to challenge the Democratic Party regulars at the national convention that fall. The accomplishments were less grand than originally envisioned but significant nonetheless. The tide was turning.

16

THE MAGNOLIA CURTAIN

During that pivotal summer another historic event loosened the segregationists' hold on power. Following a filibuster by southern senators, Congress passed the Civil Rights Act of 1964—a fitting tribute to the late President Kennedy and a watershed moment in the history of the civil rights movement. President Johnson signed the bill as part of his program for a Great Society, a vision of a nation free of widespread poverty, ignorance, and injustice. The new law prohibited segregation in places serving the general public, including restaurants, hotels, motels, playgrounds, and swimming pools. Even more important, it allowed the federal government to cut off funds to any government-supported program found to be practicing racial discrimination, including schools, hospitals, defense plants, and research labs. The threat of losing tens of millions of dollars in U.S. government funding was not lost on embattled state officials, who were finally rethinking their determination to maintain segregation "at all costs."

It was about then that Ole Miss history professor James Silver revealed to the nation the depth of the state's disdain for dissent, its censorship of books, its control of the media, and its use of secret agents to undercut civil rights. In his book *Mississippi: The Closed Society,* Silver described a state that operated more like a totalitarian police regime than a part of the modern United States of America. Silver knew firsthand of the Commission's methods through its repeated efforts to get him fired from Ole Miss. With public interest in Mississippi peaking in the wake of Freedom Summer, the book became a best seller, adding to the national pressure on the state to change its ways.

Given those pressures, the snarl of the segregationists began to ease. One of the first signs of change came from Governor Paul Johnson, who, during his campaign, had referred to the NAACP as the National Association of Apes, Coons, Niggers, and Possums. Now he was pledging to put an end to the state's support for white racism. "We are not going to be the pushing boy for that element ever again," he said. "We built the dog house we now find ourselves in." Meantime, the FBI was dismantling the Klan, and membership in the White Citizens' Council was waning, as the white middle class distanced itself from violence. The Magnolia Curtain was lifting.

CHAPTER 17

"DESTROY THIS DIRECTIVE"

By 1965, Commission director Erle Johnston was trying to reposition his segregation watchdogs as a cadre of "racial troubleshooters," a problem-solving liaison among the state government, the white community, and the black community. Seeking to rise above the reputation of a "super-snooping operation," Johnston told white civic groups that the Commission was now dedicated to negotiating solutions to disputes and intervening early to prevent misunderstandings and flare-ups. In fact, Johnston did take steps to curb the excesses of the operation. He finally cut off payments to the White Citizens' Council and became an informant to the FBI, providing valuable information for its crackdown on the Klan.

Nevertheless, the agency never really abandoned its segregationist mission—as if racism had been infused in its DNA. While publicly touting the agency as a troubleshooter, Johnston continued to play his role as the hidden protector of white rule. At one point, in a letter to a state recreation official, he recommended "closing swimming pools at the end of this summer" rather than allowing black and white children to swim together in integrated pools. His advice was not heeded. He also helped admissions officers at Mississippi Southern College force a black applicant to drop his application for admission by threatening to expose the student's sexual preference. "We have information that you are a homosexual," Johnston wrote. "If you change your mind about enrolling at an all-white university we will say no more about it. If you persist in your application, we will give this information to the press and Justice Department." The prospective student did not enroll.

That year Johnston also issued one of his most telling directives. He ordered agents to destroy documents in the Commission files. His confidential memo instructed his spies to purge their files of investigative reports that suggested interference with the voter registration process. Johnston went on to direct agents to write future reports with code words and phrases to obscure the nature of the investigations. For example, investigative reports were to refer to voting registration volunteers as "subversives," thus insulating commission agents from charges of tampering with the vote. His memo concluded, "Except for a copy being sent to the governor's office, no record of these directions will remain in our files. As soon as you have familiarized yourself with the contents, please destroy this directive." The agents destroyed the incriminating files but forgot to destroy Johnston's memo.

By 1966 Johnston was growing weary, beaten down by criticism from both sides of the racial divide. He tried unsuccessfully to persuade his superiors to change the name of the Commission to the Mississippi State Information Agency and to recast it as a modern public relations outlet. But too many powerful politicians wanted the watchdog to remain on the job. By 1967 he was arguing that the Commission had "outlived its usefulness" and was "ready for the grave." Finally, in November 1967, he announced his retirement. The state legislature thanked him for his service but refused to shut down the operation. They replaced him with a former FBI agent and maintained a skeleton staff.

Through the late 1960s, the scaled-back agency monitored school desegregation, kept tabs on anti–Vietnam War protesters, and snooped on a couple of black power groups. By the early 1970s, the powerful politicians on the Commission's governing board routinely skipped meetings, proposals to eliminate its budget came and went, and the staff was reduced to infiltrating rock concerts to spy on hippies. By summer 1973, the agency's obituary was finally being written, with the *Memphis Commercial Appeal* reporting that Mississippi's "Ole Watchdog is Barking for its Life." On July 1, 1973, the Commission staff was released, its office closed, and its records locked. Four years later the state legislature finally abolished the law that had created the Commission back in 1956.

This chapter of history was finally over. The Commission was abolished, the White Citizens' Council marginalized, and the Klan tamed. The Civil Rights Act and Voting Rights Act were the law of the land. The march toward equality and justice had picked up its pace. But the question remained: Could Mississippi really change?

In the course of researching this book, I traveled across the state contemplating that question and searching for answers. From the vast cotton fields and moss-draped bayous of the Delta to the hurricane-racked homes and glittering casinos on the Gulf Coast to the state offices and streets of Jackson, I witnessed the progress that has been made since the rule of the segregationists, when the creed of white supremacy stood as bedrock and the code of racial separation was enforced with an iron fist. The "whites only" signs are long gone from the café windows, and the storefront offices that once housed White Citizens' Council chapters have long been converted into restaurants and gift shops. Today, legions of black and white children attend school together and long lines of black and white voters stand at the polls on election day. Racial violence is a discussion topic for history students at Ole Miss rather than a frightening reality of life on that once war-torn campus.

I also saw the ghosts of the past lurking behind the signs of progress. The names of segregationist politicians are proudly etched into the granite of public buildings. Their official biographies are often cleansed of the cold, hard truth of a bygone era. These ghosts whisper that the principles of the past are still with us and remind us that history can always return as the future.

In fact, there is evidence that the bad old days are poised for a comeback. For the past two decades, public schools have been gradually resegregating as federal and state courts back off enforcement of integration laws and legislatures sidestep the issue. New white-is-right pressure groups, having resurrected the concepts of the long-defunct White Citizens' Council, target a new generation of potential race warriors on the Internet. Most details and nuances of the civil rights movement are still unknown to adults and young people today—not only in Mississippi but across the nation.

My advice is that everyone read the Commission files, with their chilling investigative reports on private citizens and their underhanded tactics for maintaining the racist status quo. In the end, the files are an important reminder of the dangers of unchecked power and the reckless disregard for individual rights. And while those files reflect the excesses of the powerful, they also reveal the strength of the people who refused to play the role of the powerless. As the investigative reports show, many of the true civil rights heroes were ordinary folks who hailed from the small towns and clapboard shacks of the Magnolia State, who carried on their struggle to bring down segregation and discrimination with the constant shadow of the state looming over them. Their names—categorized in the files as race agitators, subversives, and communists—live on as champions of the most powerful democratic movement in our history.

WHAT HAPPENED NEXT

The Commission files: The end of the Commission started a heated debate over the fate of the six locked file cabinets of secret papers that had been removed from the office and stored in an underground vault. Resisting calls from lawmakers to destroy the files altogether, the legislature voted to keep the documents sealed for another 50 years, until July 1, 2027. The American Civil Liberties Union filed suit demanding the documents be opened to the public without delay. The courts finally ordered the files to be made public, and their release in 1998 revealed the extent of the secret enterprise.

The FBI: Director J. Edgar Hoover carried out his orders to defuse Klan violence in Mississippi but proved no friend to the civil rights movement. By the mid-1960s Hoover was pressing ahead with COINTELPRO—a massive federal spying operation targeting civil rights advocates, anti-war groups, and alleged communists. The bureau's use of electronic eavesdropping, master-ful sabotage, and extensive infiltration took the art of domestic spying to a dangerous new level.

Agent X: The Day Detective Agency operated a string of black agents for the Commission. The reports were filed under the code name Informant X to protect the identity of the operatives. A comprehensive review of the Commission's files indicates that a primary operative infiltrated the organizations that were planning Mississippi Freedom Summer in 1964 and provided a steady stream of intelligence to the Commission. The information was passed on to law enforcement and fell into the hands of the Ku Klux Klan.

Following the release of the Commission papers, civil rights activists were particularly interested in answering this question: Who was the Agent X who compromised Mississippi Freedom Summer? A number of activists pointed to R. L. Bolden, who had attended infiltrated meetings, worked on compromised campaigns, and been at the scene of the Freedom Summer training seminars in Ohio. In an interview for this book, Bolden conceded that he worked with the Day Agency and admitted that he provided his bosses with details of civil rights meetings. He insisted the information he passed along was public and claimed there were no secrets in the wide-open civil rights movement. Acknowledging that the Day Agency may have passed his information on to the Commission, he added, "I was not the only one."

Erle Johnston: After retiring from the Commission, Johnston returned to his hometown, edited his weekly newspaper, and authored a number of books, including a reminiscence about segregationist governor Ross Barnett titled *I Rolled with Ross.* Through the years,

Johnston seemed conflicted between the romance of operating near the height of state power and the shame of doing the bidding of the white power structure. Following the release of the commission files, Johnston came under criticism for the agency's excesses, and his claims of being a "practical segregationist" and "troubleshooter" failed to dissuade his detractors. He sat on a board dedicated to the preservation of historic papers for Tougaloo College, which he once spied on. He died in 1995.

J. P. Coleman: After leaving the governor's office, Coleman went on to a distinguished career in government. Driven by a passion for public service, he ran for and won a seat in the state legislature in 1960 and was appointed a federal judge in 1965. He served on the federal court for 16 years. His legacy would always be compromised by the stroke of his pen that created the Sovereignty Commission. He died in 1991.

Aaron Henry: Persevering in his fight for integration and voting rights, Henry served as a community organizer, coalition builder, and respected leader. He was elected to the Mississippi State Legislature in 1982 and served until 1996. He died in 1997.

Clyde Kennard: After he succumbed to cancer in 1963, Kennard's attempt to integrate Mississippi Southern College was reduced to a footnote in civil rights history. But then students at Lincolnshire High School in Illinois, along with the Center for Wrongful Convictions

at Northwestern University, persuaded Kennard's ac-
cuser to recant the testimony that had led to Kennard's
conviction as an accomplice to the theft of five bags of
chicken feed. In 2006 a judge in the same courtroom
where Kennard had been found guilty back in 1960
vacated his conviction. In addition, a building has
been named in his honor at the University of Southern
Mississippi, formerly Mississippi Southern College.

Ross Barnett: After leaving the governor's office in
1964, Barnett suffered a decline in popularity as word of
his secret dealings with the Kennedys spread. He failed
in a second bid for the governor's office and faded from
public view. He was reduced to speaking at white supremacist gatherings and playing accordion and telling
stories at county fairs. He died in 1987.

James Meredith: After graduating from Ole Miss,
Meredith was shot while leading a March Against Fear
from Memphis to Jackson in 1966. Dr. Martin Luther
King and other civil rights leaders continued the march
for him, and Meredith recovered from his wounds and re-
joined the trek. Years later, in a dramatic shift, Meredith
became a stockbroker, a member of the Republican
Party, and a staff member of archconservative Senator
Jesse Helms. He claimed that liberal Democrats were the
greatest enemies of African Americans. He also wrote an
11-volume history of Mississippi. In 1997 he donated his
personal papers to Ole Miss.

Byron De La Beckwith: After walking away free from two trials in the shooting death of Medgar Evers, "Delay Beckwith" went on to play a leadership role in white supremacist groups. In 1994, De La Beckwith was retried for the murder of Medgar Evers amid revelations that the Commission had intervened for the defense during the second trial. This time a jury of eight blacks and four whites found him guilty, and a judge sentenced him to life at Parchman Farm. He died in prison in 2001.

Percy Greene: Scorned as a sellout by many in the black community, Greene finally sold his newspaper and retired. As activist Fred Clark recalled, "They were paying him for those articles that he would write about black people. . . .He was wearing fine suits, smoking the best cigars, but deep down inside people around him didn't like him because of how he was getting his money, off the blood of the black people. But he had suffered himself and just didn't see no light or no hope at the end of the tunnel."

SELECTED DOCUMENTS FROM THE ARCHIVES OF THE MISSISSIPPI STATE SOVEREIGNTY COMMISSION

TRICKERY TREACHERY TYRANNY and TREASON in Washington

Pamphlet opposing
civil rights reform in
Washington

THIS REQUISITION MAY BE HANDLED THROUGH BANKING CHANNELS AS A CHECK

State of Mississippi

THE

№ 338

REQUISITION on the Auditor of Public Accounts   JACKSON, MISSISSIPPI March 28   19 57

PAY TO H. M. Simes $ 175.00

One Hundred Seventy-Five and no/100 _____DOLLARS

ACCOUNT OF **STATE SOVEREIGNTY COMMISSION**

For Investigation for Sovereignty Commission   Chapter 97, Laws 1956

PAY PERIOD	GROSS PAY	TAX	S. S.	RET.	INS.	OTHERS

CHAIRMAN

DETACH BEFORE DEPOSITING

Pay Period	Gross Pay	Tax	S. S.	Ret.	Ins.	Others	Check

THIS REQUISITION MAY BE HANDLED THROUGH BANKING CHANNELS AS A CHECK

State of Mississippi

THE

№ 219

REQUISITION on the Auditor of Public Accounts   JACKSON, MISSISSIPPI October 16, 19 56

PAY TO Mutual Association of Colored People South - C/o Percy Green $ 200.00

Two hundred and no/100 _____DOLLARS

ACCOUNT OF **STATE SOVEREIGNTY COMMISSION**

For_____   Chapter 97, Laws 1956

PAY PERIOD	GROSS PAY	TAX	S. S.	RET.	INS.	OTHERS

CHAIRMAN

DETACH BEFORE DEPOSITING

Pay Period	Gross Pay	Tax	S. S.	Ret.	Ins.	Others	Check

№ 219

Commission checks to compensate black collaborators
for services rendered

July 6, 1959

MEMO TO: File

FROM: Zack J. Van Landingham

SUBJECT: NAACP Meeting, Jackson, Mississippi, May 17, 1959.

At the above named meeting at which Roy Wilkins spoke, the Police Department furnished the following list of license tags around the negro Masonic Temple where the meeting was held. The names and addresses were obtained through a check with the Motor Vehicle Registration Bureau, Jackson, Mississippi.

COUNTY	LICENSE	AUTO	NAME	ADDRESS
Hinds	388-005	53 Ford	Huey David Thompson, Rt. 1, Jackson	
Holmes	427-813	56 Ford	Wilson Tate, Thornton, Miss.	
Madison	639-941	51 Chevrolet	Rudolph Coats, Canton, Miss.	
Hinds	366-503	53 Chevrolet	Preston Phillips, 724 Adams St., Jackson	
Hinds	384-869	56 Plymouth	Hunter Sharp, 1104 Plymouth Ave., Jackson	
Rankin	771-432	54 Lincoln	A. B. Terrell, Rt. 6, Box 115	
Hinds	385-508	49 Kaiser	James W. Spencer, 4674 Cedar Hurst, Jackson	
Hinds	372-826	49 Chevrolet	Caldonia Jackson, 1233 Hill St., Jackson	
Jeff Davis	477-446	52 Buick	H. D. Darby, Prentiss, Mississippi	
Monroe	673-125	57 Oldsmobile	Roosevelt Annison, Amory, Miss.	
Oktibbeha	705-142	53 Chrysler	W. L. Mitchell, State College, Miss.	
Claiborne	F/62-305	52 Chevrolet	William Owens, Pattison, Miss.	
Tunica	840-838	56 Chevrolet	Isaac Fields, Tunica, Miss.	
Rankin	771-724	53 Ford	Wardell Sanders, Rt. 1, Florence, Miss.	
Rankin	F/5 67-516	56 Ford	Robert Griffith, Rt. 3, Brandon, Miss.	
Hinds	397-894	52 Chrysler	Mattie S. Rundles, 159 E. Bell St., Jackson	
Hinds	382-459	54 Chevrolet	Fred Evans, Clinton, Miss.	
Hinds	366-376	56 Chevrolet	Florence Carter, 3816 Wabash Street, Jackson	
Hinds	378-231	55 Mercury	Cora S. Reed, 2130 Guynes, Jackson	
Hinds	391-717	48 Kaiser	S. L. Bass, 1611 N. Lamar, Jackson	
Hinds	360-810	57 Buick	W. J. Summers, 619 W. Pearl, Jackson	
Hinds	370-878	53 Chevrolet	Bessie M. Walker, 1007 Lynch St., Jackson	
Hinds	388-753	50 Ford	C. L. Lee, 268, George St., Jackson	
Hinds	389-682	50 Ford	Samuel A. Cotten, 5432 Gault St., Jackson	
Yazoo	930-473	50 Pontiac	Sam Knight, Rt. 2, Box 315, Yazoo City, Miss.	
Washington	891-301	56 Pontiac	Jessie Lee Carter, Greenville, Miss.	
Hinds	365-379	55 Oldsmobile	H. M. Ross, 118 Horseshoe Circle, Jackson	
George	280-193	57 Oldsmobile	Claude D. Phillips, Lucedale, Miss.	
Pike	735-586	50 Pontiac	Hubert Lee Gayden, McComb, Miss.	
Forrest	253-715	58 Mercury	Clyde Kennard, Rt. 1, Hattiesburg, Miss.	
Rankin	769-483	55 Ford	Henry Lewis, Rt. 2, Florence, Miss.	
Lauderdale	527-205	56 Chevrolet	Cozy Houston, 1113-32nd Ave., Meridian, Miss.	
Hinds	357-113	51 Pontiac	Doshie Bridge, 2245 Whitfield, Jackson	
Hinds	375-618	57 Ford	Robert R. Beasley, 737 Robinson, Jackson	
Hinds	373-588	50 Pontiac	Robert L. Littleton, 828 Detroit, Jackson	
Hinds	382-387	53 Chrysler	J. T. Naugher, 335 Briarwood, Jackson	
Hinds	355-396	56 Pontiac	James L. Waits, Jr., 1217 Florence, Jackson	
Hinds	357-745	56 Pontiac	Robert L. Ford, 1624 Hill St., Jackson	
Jasper	471-446	53 Buick	Not reported as of May	
Warren	862-260	55 Chevrolet	David Kent, 512 Farmer, Vicksburg, Miss.	
Sunflower	805-705	53 Chevrolet	James Holman, Drew, Miss.	
Harrison	327-249	59 Chevrolet	Bessie H. Parker, 519-16th St., Miss. City, Mis	
		58 Volkswagen	Not Set	
Hinds	351-738	50 Pontiac	Paul Carter, 220 Englewood, Jackson	

2-5-154

Extensive lists of license plate numbers of suspected NAACP members

Memo To: Zack J. VanLandingham, Chief Investigator

From: M. L. Malone, Director

Subject: Chiropractor's School, Ft. Worth, Texas

On September 25, 1959, I received a telephone call from
Dr. David Perkins, Chiropractor of Jackson, Mississippi,
whose telephone number is FL 5-6333. He stated that a
Chiropractor's school was held in the Hilton Hotel, Ft.
Worth, Texas on September 17, 18, 19, and 20, 1959, and
that upon arriving at the class, he found a Negro in
attendance to take the courses; that he objected to attending
classes with a Negro and refused to participate.

He stated that the following Chiropractors attended the
classes from Mississippi:

Dr. R. W. Tyer, North West Street, Jackson, Mississippi;
Dr. Glenn F. Glenn, North West Street, Jackson, Mississippi;
Dr. John P. Charles, North West Street, Jackson, Mississippi;
Dr. L. A. Norville, Jr., North West Street, Jackson, Mississippi;
Dr. Wheeler Johnson, Greenville, Mississippi; Dr. Billy
Johnson, Greenwood, Mississippi; Dr. Jack Cleer, Hattiesburg,
Mississippi; Dr. F. L. Cooper, Carthage, Mississippi; Dr. Jimmy
Barfoot, Philadelphia, Mississippi.

Dr. Perkins stated that some of these men were integrationists,
but none of them apparently objected to attending classes with
the Negro.

September 30, 1959

*Memo alerting the Commission of an
integrated chiropractor class*

PUBLIC EDUCATION IS A FUNCTION OF THE STATES AND NOT THE FEDERAL GOVERNMENT.

Five times the U. S. Supreme Court ruled that separate but equal facilities for education are not violative of the constitution. In May, 1954, the court reversed itself—YET THE CONSTITUTION HAD NOT BEEN CHANGED, NO AMENDMENT HAD BEEN SUBMITTED TO THE STATE OR TO THE PEOPLE, AND THE CONSTITUTION ITSELF SPECIFICALLY RESERVES TO THE STATES THOSE POWERS NOT EXPRESSLY GRANTED TO THE FEDERAL GOVERNMENT.

Mississippi believes in the rights of the states to solve many of their own internal problems. Mississippi would not presume to solve the problems of the Asiatics on the west coast, the Mexicans in the southwest, the Latins on the east coast, or the Indians in the middle west. Mississippi believes it is up to those people living nearest the problems to solve them in moral and ethical manner, without interference or coercive action from the federal government.

The heavy ratio of Negro population to whites in Mississippi—42 to 58 per cent—has inspired a social system of segregation under which both races make progress without forced associations which might create suspicion and chaos and retard the progress now being made. White and Negro leaders, working together in an atmosphere of mutual cooperation, trust, and good will, can solve Mississippi's racial problems without pressures from courts, law-making groups, or professional agitators.

President Abraham Lincoln, The Great Emancipator, was aware of the racial problems when he told a group of 500 Negroes at Washington, D. C., on August 14, 1862:

"You and we are different races. We have between us a broader difference than exists between almost any other two races. Whether it be right or wrong, I need not discuss; but this physical difference is a great disadvantage to us both. Your race suffers by living among us, while ours suffers from your presence. In a word, we suffer on each side. If this be admitted, it affords a reason, at least, why we should be separated."

MISSISSIPPI
IS
EDUCATING
...WITHOUT
INTEGRATING

This pamphlet prepared by:
PUBLIC RELATIONS DEPARTMENT

THE MISSISSIPPI STATE SOVEREIGNTY COMMISSION

Governor Ross Barnett, Chairman
JACKSON, MISS.

Pamphlet designed to show how the state provided quality segregated schools for black children

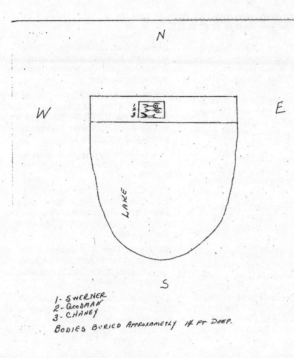

N

W   E

LAKE

S

1- SWERNER
2- GOODMAN
3- CHANEY
BODIES BURIED APPROXAMETLY 14 FT DEEP.

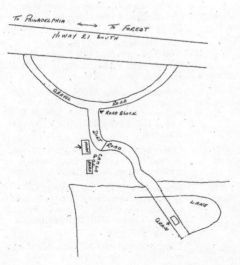

To PHILADELPHIA ⟷ To FOREST
HIWAY 21 SOUTH

GRAVEL

ROAD

← ROAD BLOCK

DIRT ROAD

HOUSE

CANLOE PLACE

LAKE

CRANE

Hand-drawn map supplied by Commission agent Andy Hopkins depicting the site where FBI agents discovered the bodies of three civil rights workers. The sketch indicates that the bodies were discovered 14 feet deep in an earthen dam.

BIBLIOGRAPHY

Many of the sources for this book include specific investigative reports from the Mississippi State Sovereignty Commission (MSSC). Specific citations are listed below. Maintained by the Mississippi Department of Archives and History (MDAH), many of the reports can be accessed online at http://mdah.state.ms.us/.

"Aaron Henry Case Reflects Mississippi Racial Conflict," *Daily Corinthian* (Corinth, MS), October 8, 1964.

"Appeal Lost by Kennard," *Jackson Democrat*. October 9, 1961. SCR ID# 10-28-0-15-1-1-1. MDAH. Digital Archives.

Agent X Reports: February 23, 1964, SCR ID # 9-31-1-9-1-1-1; March 24, 1964, SCR ID # 9-31-1-27-1-1-1; May 14, SCR ID # 9-31-1-29-1-1-1; 1964, June 9, 1964, SCR ID # 9-31-1-70-1-1-1; June 16, 1964, SCR ID # 9-31-1-74-1-1-1; June 16, 17, 18, 1964, SCR ID # 9-31-1-73 -1-1-1. MDAH. Digital Archives.

Barnett, Ross. Inaugural Address, *Journal of Mississippi House of Representatives, 1960*, regular session. MDAH.

Barnett, Ross. Television address to State of Mississippi, Sept 13, 1962. American Radio Works: http://americanradioworks.publicradio.org/features/prestapes/barnettspeech.html.

Bolden, R. L. Personal interview, Jackson, MS, March 2009. Conducted by Rick Bowers.

"Box Score of Freedom Riders Arrests and Convictions." *Jackson Daily News*. July 7, 1961.

Brady, Thomas Pickens. *Black Monday*. 2nd ed. Winona, WI: Association of Citizens' Councils of Mississippi, 1955.

"Judge Tosses Out 1960 Conviction: Students Work to Clear Man's Name," *Chicago Tribune*. May 18, 2006.

Civil Rights Act of 1964 (Public Law 88-352). Passed July 2, 1964.

Civil Rights in Mississippi, University of Southern Mississippi Digital Archive. McCain Library and Archives. http://www.lib.usm.edu/legacy/spcol/crda/.

Clark, Fred. Oral history interview June 10, 1994. University of Southern Mississippi, USM Digital Archive. http://www.lib.usm.edu/legacy/spcol/crda/oh/index.html.

"Clyde Kennard Dies in Chicago Hospital," *Jackson Daily News*. July 5, 1963.

Cobb, James C. The Most *Southern Place on Earth – The Mississippi Delta and the Roots of Regional Identity*. New York: Oxford University Press, 1992.

Coleman, Gov. J. P. James P. Coleman Papers, *Journal of the House of Representatives,* 1956, regular session. MDAH.

Crespino, Joseph. *In Search of Another Country: Mississippi and the Conservative Counterrevolution*. Princeton, NJ: Princeton University Press, 2007.

DeCell, Hal. MSSC. 6 January 1958. SCR ID # 9-0-0-40-1-1-1, SCR ID# 1-16-1-1-1-1-1 to 1-16-1-18-1-1-1. MDAH Digital Archives.

Delaughter, Bobby. *Never Too Late: A Prosecutor's Story of Justice in the Medgar Evers Case*. New York: Scribner, 2001.

Dittmer, John. *Local People: The Struggle for Civil Rights in Mississippi*. Champaign: University of Illinois Press, 1994.

Downing, Virgil. MSSC Investigator. February 14, 1961, SCR ID# 1-67-1-2-1-1-1; February 26, 1964, SCR ID# 2-112-1-36-1-1-1. MDAH. Digital Archives.

"Elections: Mississippi Mud," *Time*, September 7, 1959. http://www.jfklibrary.org/meredith/index.htm.

Ely, James W. Jr. and Bradley G. Bond, eds. "Profiles of Ross Barnett and Theodore Bilbo," *Law & Politics* (2008). Chapel Hill: University of North Carolina.

Evers, Myrlie and Marable Manning.

The Autobiography of Medgar Evers: A Hero's Life and Legacy Revealed Through His Writings, Letters, and Speeches. New York: Basic Civitas Books, 2005.

—with William Peters. *For Us, The Living, the Widow of Civil Rights Leader Medgar Evers Tells the Story of Their Life Together in Mississippi and of His Tragic Assassination.* New York: Doubleday, 1967.

"Featured Project," Bluhm Legal Clinic: News and Notes, p. 4. Northwestern University School of Law, Fall 2006. http://www.law. northwestern.edu/legalclinic/news/newlttrarchive/Fall06.pdf.

Finley, Melissa. *But I Was a Practical Segregationist: Erle Johnston and the Mississippi State Sovereignty Commission,* Master's Thesis. University of Southern Mississippi, 2000.

Frankhauser, David. *Freedom Rides: Recollections of David Frankhauser.* Online at http://biology.clc.uc.edu/Frankhauser/index.htm.

General Laws of the State of Mississippi, Chapter 365, 520–524 (1956).

Henry, Aaron and Constance Curry. *Aaron Henry: The Fire Ever Burning.* Jackson: University Press of Mississippi, 2000.

"High Court Rejects Appeal by Kennard," *Clarion Ledger.* October 10, 1961, SCR ID# 10-28-0-15-1-1-1. MDAH. Digital Archives.

Hopkins, A. L., December 4, 1958, SCR# 3-74-1-17-3-1-1; February 9, 1961, SCR ID# 2-55-1-77-1-1-1; June 30 1961, SCR ID # 2-55-3-29-1-1-1; April 9, 1964, SCR# 1-77-0-19-1-1-1; June 29, 1964, SCR ID # 2-112-1-41-1-1-1, # 2-112-1-44-1-1-1; August 13, 1964, SCR # 2-112-1-19-1-1-1; August 25, 1964, SCR # 2-112-1-42-1-1-1, April 8, 1965, SCR# 6-36-0-51-2-1-1, SCR ID # 2-112-1-51-1-1-1, SCR ID # 2-112-1-50-1-1-1. MDAH. Digital Archives.

Humes, Henry Harrison, SCR ID # 1-0-0-18-1-1-1- to 99-95-0-13-1-1-1; SCR ID# 97-104-0-75-1-1-1; SCR ID# 97-104-0-77-3-1-1. MDAH. Digital Archive

Johnston, Erle. Interviews conducted July 30, 1980, and August 13, 1993. *Civil Rights in Mississippi Digital Archive.* University of Southern Mississippi. http://www.lib.usm.edu/~spcol/crda/oh/index.html.

—A Report of the First 18 Months of the Public Relations Program, 1962, SCR ID# 99-139-0-1-1-1-1; February 8, 1965, SCR ID # 99-62-0-33-1-1-1. MDAH. Digital Archives.

— *I Rolled with Ross.* Forest, MS: Lake Harbor Publishers, 1980.

Katagiri, Yasuhiro. *The Mississippi State Sovereignty Commission: Civil Rights and States Rights.* Jackson: University Press of Mississippi, 2001.

Kennard, Clyde. Editorial. *Hattiesburg American* (Hattiesburg, MS), December 6, 1958.

Kennedy, Randall. *Sellout: The Politics of Racial Betrayal.* New York: Vintage Books, 2009.

Levitas, Daniel. *The Terrorist Next Door: The Militia Movement and the Radical Right.* New York: St. Martin's Press, 2002.

Maass, Peter. "The Secrets of Mississippi, Post Authoritarian Shock in the South." *The New Republic.* December 21, 1998.

Mars, Florence and Lynn Eden. *Witness in Philadelphia.* Baton Rouge: Louisiana State University Press, 1977.

The Message from Mississippi (film). MSSC. July 1960. MDAH. Digital Archives.

Mississippi is Educating... Without Integrating (pamphlet). MSSC. MDAH. Resource Room File.

"Moderation Stand Gives Negro Leaders Humes, Green Hot Time," *Delta Democrat Times* (Greenville, MS), July 28, 1957.

MSSC. Sovereignty Commission records on formation of investigative function, SCR ID # 7-0-1-56-1-1-1 to SCR ID# 7-0-1-56-12-1-1; June 12, 1957, SCR# 10-0-1-108-1-1, SCR # 7-3-0-1-6-1-1; July 13, 1959, SCR ID# 7-0-1-56-1-1-1 to 7-0-1-56- 12-1-1; July 6, 1961, SCR ID # 2-140-3-37-1-1-1; October 31, 1962, SCR # ID 97-11-0-222-1-1-1; MDAH. Digital Archives.

NAACP. "About the NAACP: History." http://www.naacp.org/about/history/index.htm.

—New Member Card, #SCR ID 9-31-2-5-6-1-1. MDAH. Digital Archives.

"Negro Claims He Wants to Enroll at Mississippi Southern College," *Meridian Star*, Meridian, MS, Dec. 11, 1958.

"Negroes to Pursue Vote," *Daily Times Leader*, West Point, MS, November 17, 1958.

"No Cadillacking About—Negro Editor Challenges King to Make Himself a Martyr," *Jackson Daily News*, July 6, 1961.

"No God—Non-Christian Freedom Riders Learn Trade in Red School," *Jackson Clarion Ledger*, June 30, 1961.

Nossiter, Adam. *Of Long Memory: Mississippi and the Murder of Medgar Evers*. Reading, MA: Addison-Wesley, 1995.

Operator #79. March 15, 1964. SCR ID # 9-31-1-22-1-1-1. MDAH. Digital Archives.

Orr-Klopfer, M. Susan, Fred Klopfer, and Berry Klopfer. *Where Rebels Roost: Mississippi Civil Rights Revisited*. M. Susan Orr-Klopfer: 2005.

Percy, William Alexander, *Lanterns on the Levee: Recollections of a Planter's Son,* Baton Rouge: Louisiana State University Press, 1941.

"Riders Ties to Commies," *Jackson Clarion Ledger*. July 2, 1961.

"Rifle Fingerprint Called Beckwith's," *Jackson Daily News*. Feb. 3, 1964.

Peterson, Jason A., "Forgotten and Ignored: Mississippi Newspaper Coverage of Clyde Kennard and His Effort to Integrate Mississippi Southern College." Paper presented to the Association for Education in Journalism. August 2006.

Rosenberg, Gerald N. *The Hollow Hope: Can Courts Bring Social Change?* Urbana, IL: University of Chicago Press, 1991.

Scarborough, Tom, Oct 9 1962, SCR ID # 2-19-0-23-1-1-1. MDAH. Digital Archives.

Silver, James W. *Mississippi: The Closed Society*. London: Gollancz, 1964.

St. John Barrett, U.S. Department of Justice—Civil Rights Division. *A Personal Memoir 2008*.

"Soviets Planned Freedom Rides, State Officials Tell of Havana Seminar," *Jackson Daily News,* June 29, 1961.

"State Proves Negro's Guilt," *Memphis Commercial Appeal,* September 30, 1959.

"The Message from Mississippi" (speech), July 1960. MDAH.

"The South: Trouble in Alabama," *Time*, May 26, 1961. http://www.time.com/time/magazine/article/0,9171,872446,00.html.

"Sovereignty Commission Online Agency History." Digital Collections. MDAH.

Tucker, William H. *The Funding of Scientific Racism, Wickliffe Draper and the Pioneer Fund*. Urbana: University of Illinois Press, 2002.

Van Landingham, Zach C. Aug. 30, 1958, SCR ID # 1-16-1-21-1-1-1 to 1-16-1-21-1-1-1; Dec. 17, 1958, SCR ID #1-27-0-6-1-1-1 to 1-27-0-6-37-1-1; May 6, 1959, SCR ID# 5-3-1-19-1-1-1; September 21, 1959, SCR ID #1-27-0-40-1-1-1 to 1-27-0-41-6-1-1-1, SCR ID# 1-27-0-41-1-1-1. MDAH. Digital Archives. Report to the State Legislature on the early activities of the Sovereignty Commission. SCR ID # 7-3-0-5-1-1-1 to 7-3-0-8-1-1-1. MDAH. Digital Archives.

Waldron, Ann. *Hodding Carter: The Reconstruction of a Racist*. Chapel Hill, NC: Algonquin Books, 1993.

Watner, Callia and Anya. "Clyde Kennard: Gone but Not Forgotten," *Justice Denied: The Magazine for the Wrongly Convicted*, Summer 2006, no. 33. http://justicedenied.org/issue/issue_33/jd_issue_33.pdf.

Williams, Julian. "Percy Greene and the Mississippi State Sovereignty Commission." *Journalism History* 28, no. 2 (Summer 2002). University of Southern Mississippi Archive.

QUOTE SOURCES

P 3: "maintain the continued separation..." and "no task for..." Coleman inaugural address, p 67; P 4: "fire-eaters" Finely, p 9. P 7: "with all deliberate speed" *Brown* v. *Board* implementation decree. P 9: "When the pot..." Carter. P 11: "vicious falsehoods" and "poison pens" Katagiri, p 9. P 15: "seeking out intelligence..." MSSC SCR 7-0-1-6-2-1-1. P 16: "this problem will never..." and "a large number of fine..." Katagiri, p 37. P 17: "vindictive speeches..." Williams, p 3. P 19: "quick to get their..." and "fallen into..." Katagiri, p 42. P 19-20: "unworthy..." Katagiri, p 42. P 20: "The death of..." and "remove all files" DeCell, SCR 9-0-0-40-1-1. P 23: "the most Southern..." Cobb, title page. P 25: "You know that old..." Curry, p xiv; "it is believed..." Van Landingham, SCR 1-16-1-21-1-1-1 to 1-16-1-21-1-1-1. P 26: "advised that he..." Van Landingham, SCR 1-16-1-21-1-1-1. P 28-29: "Are we to assume..." Kennard. P 29: "The Clyde Kennard problem..." Katagiri, p 60; "Persons who know..." Van Landingham, SCR 1-27-06-1-1-1. P 30: "The files of..." and "take care of him..." Van Landingham, SCR 1-27-06-1-1-1. P 32: "appeared to be frame up" Dittmer, p 82. P 35: "May the good Lord..." Crespino, p 35. P 37: "You know and I know..." Barnett, Inaugural Address, p 51. P 38: "God is the ultimate segregationist..." Barnett obituary, *NY Times,* Nov. 7, 1987; "fine Christian fellowship" Crespino, p 16. P 40: "utterances or actions..." Katagiri, p 89. P 41: "This is a selling..." Katagiri, p 76. P 42: "which showed in words..." Katagiri, p 82. P 43: "never, never land," U.S. Court of Appeals, Fifth Circuit, *Meredith* v *Fair*, Jan. 12, 1962. P 45: "the extremely poor prognosis..." Dittmer, p 82. P 47: "I'm taking a ride..." Katagiri, p 96. P 48: "I'm going out..." Frankhauser. P 51: "filling the jails" Colson, 397. P 52: "He said: Come take my mattress...." and "A guard came in..." Frankhauser. P 53: "self styled..." Katagiri, p 97. P 54: "They're pawns..." *Jackson Daily News,* June 29, 1961. P 57-58: RFK and Barnett, federal transcript, Sept 25, 1962. P 58: "caddillacking around," *Jackson Daily News,* July 6, 1961; "What were you in jail for..." St. John Barrett, personal memoir. P 61: "known Cap Meredith..." and "Mr. Coleman also..." Downing,

SCR 1-67-1-2-1-1-1-1; "Meredith Drives Cadillac..." *Jackson Clarion Ledger,* June 16, 1961. P 62: "a carefully calculated..." U.S. Court of Appeals, Fifth Circuit, (306 F.2d 374) July 27, 1962; "unnatural warfare..." MSSC, SCR 97-11-0-222-1-1-1; "our greatest crisis..." Barnett, Television address. P 63: "Which one of you..." Katagiri, p 108. P 64: "If there is to be..." Katagiri, p 110. P 64-65: "I was under..." RFK and Barnett, federal transcript, Sept 27, 1962. P 66: "I love Mississippi..." and "I looked back..." Dittmer, p 140; "As he stood..." Johnston, *I Rolled with Ross.* P 67: "you had an agreement..." and "that won't do at all..." RFK and Barnett, federal transcript, Sept. 30, 1962. P 68: "My heart says..." Barnett, Television address. P 69: "It is my opinion..." Scarborough. P 72: "quiet integrationist," Nossiter, p 28. P 74: He is a weak..." Hopkins, SCR 74-1-17-3-1-1 1; "Evers spoke" MSSC SCR 2-5-2-95-1-1-1; "The NAACP is..." MSSC SCR 2-72-2-58-1-1-1. P 76: "practically jumped up." *Jackson Daily News*, Feb. 3, 1964, p 1; "Expert with a pistol..." Associated Press, Jan. 23, 2001. P 78: "believed to be..." Hopkins, SCR 1-77-0-19-1-1-1. P 80: "to lay plans for..." Katagiri, p 122. P 81: "The difference between..." Tucker, p 286. P 84: "Peace Corp–type operation," Agent X, SCR 9-31-1-9-1-1-1; "The program of voter registration..." Agent X, SCR 9-31-1-1-22-1-1-1. P 85: "It appears now" and "completely integrated..." and "After a few interviews..." Agent X, SCR 9-31-1-37-1-1-1; "I decided..." Agent X, SCR 9-31-1-67-1-1-1. P 85-86: "X is departing..." MSSC, SCR 9-31-1-74-1-1-1. P 86: "Now get this..." Klopfer, p 423. P 87: "The purpose of..." Katagiri, p 159. P 87: "communists, sex perverts..." Downing, SCR 2-112-1-36-1-1-1. P 88: "secret organizations of..." Crespino, p 115; "The first contact..." Crespino, p 112. P 92: "these subjects met..." and "There are rumors..." Hopkins, SCR 2-111-1-41-1-1-1 to 1-19-1-1-1. P 93: "Cuba or another" *Jackson Clarion Ledger* editorial, Aug. 3, 1964. P 96: "We are not going to be" Crespino, p 118. P 98: "We have evidence..." Finley; "Except for a copy..." Johnston, SCR 99-62-0-33-1-1-1. P 99: "Ole Watchdog Is..." Katagiri, 225.

INDEX